Numerology Explained

Basics of Numerology, Life Path Numbers, Destiny Expression Numbers, Personal Year Numbers, Master Numbers, Calculations and More!

By Riley Star

Copyrights and Trademarks

All rights reserved. No part of this book may be reproduced or transformed in any form or by any means, graphic, electronic, or mechanical, including photocopying, recording, taping, or by any information storage retrieval system, without the written permission of the author.

This publication is Copyright ©2019. Nevada. All products, graphics, publications, software and services mentioned and recommended in this publication are protected by trademarks. In such instance, all trademarks & copyright belong to the respective owners. For information consult www.NRBpublishing.com

Disclaimer and Legal Notice

This product is not legal, medical, or accounting advice and should not be interpreted in that manner. You need to do your own due-diligence to determine if the content of this product is right for you. While every attempt has been made to verify the information shared in this publication, neither the author, neither publisher, nor the affiliates assume any responsibility for errors, omissions or contrary interpretation of the subject matter herein. Any perceived slights to any specific person(s) or organization(s) are purely unintentional.

We have no control over the nature, content and availability of the web sites listed in this book. The inclusion of any web site links does not necessarily imply a recommendation or endorse the views expressed within them. We take no responsibility for, and will not be liable for, the websites being temporarily unavailable or being removed from the internet.

The accuracy and completeness of information provided herein and opinions stated herein are not guaranteed or warranted to produce any particular results, and the advice and strategies, contained herein may not be suitable for every individual. Neither the author nor the publisher shall be liable for any loss incurred as a consequence of the use and application, directly or indirectly, of any information presented in this work. This publication is designed to provide information in regard to the subject matter covered. Neither the author nor the publisher assume any responsibility for any errors or omissions, nor do they represent or warrant that the ideas, information, actions, plans, suggestions contained in this book is in all cases accurate. It is the reader's responsibility to find advice before putting anything written in this book into practice. The information in this book is not intended to serve as legal, medical, or accounting advice.

Foreword

Numerology is the ancient system and practice of observing numbers as this could give meaning to one's life or provide direction to the 'right' path. This ancient practice uncovers numbers in all reality that has to do with one's date of birth and other significant information such as one's name, age, zodiac sign etc. All of this information can be used in numerology as it could illuminate an individual's life path, and most importantly one's purpose.

The ancient system of numerology dares back during the ancient civilization including Babylon, Atlantis, and Egypt. For our ancestors, they believe that each person born in this world has a purpose and a plan. They believe that we can all come close to this plan or discover our true purpose with the aid of numerology. All we have to do is to learn the system, and be aware of what the universe is communicating to us through the numbers we see so that we can interpret it and possibly draw meaning out of it.

For our ancestors and for most people, we are all created by an infinite Being making us an important part of Creation. Everything has a message whether it is incorporated in the code of our genetic make – up, through other ancient practices, spirit guides and the likes. The messages through numerology or other ancient systems are all written in the fabric of creation and its main purpose is to help all of us to help us stay in our supposed path or illuminate it moving forward.

There are different methods used in order to practice this ancient system. You can learn your life path number, destiny number, soul number, personality number and the likes. These are all brought together to create a personality numerology profile so that you can understand yourself better and the reality in which you live so that you can move forward. This book will guide you on how you can use numerology and find out how this ancient wisdom and knowledge can help you in knowing what the universe is telling you through numerology.

Table of Contents

Introduction 1

Chapter One: Basics of Numerology: Life Path Number, Destiny Expression Number and Personal Year Number 2

    Life Path Number 3

    Destiny Expression Number 6

    Calculating Your Personal Year Number 9

Chapter Two: Life Path Numbers 1, 2 and 3 12

    Life Path Number 1: The Leader 13

    Life Path Number 2: The Mediator 22

    Life Path Number 3: The Communicator 28

Chapter Three: Life Path Numbers 4, 5 and 6 34

    Life Path Number 5: The Freedom Seeker 39

    Life Path Number 6: The Nurturer 44

Chapter Four: Life Path Numbers 7, 8 and 9 50

    Life Path Number 7: The Seeker 50

    Life Path Number 8: The Powerhouse 56

    Life Path Number 9: The Humanitarian 60

Chapter Five: Master Numbers 11, 22 and 33 66

    Master Number 11 66

    Master Number 22 70

    Master Number 33 72

Chapter Six: Destiny Expression Numbers 1, 2, 3 and 4 76

    Destiny Expression Number 1 76

    Destiny Expression Number 2 78

    Destiny Expression Number 3 80

    Destiny Expression Number 4 82

Chapter Seven: Destiny Expression Numbers 5, 6, 7, 8 and 9 86

    Destiny Expression Number 5 86

    Destiny Expression Number 6 88

    Destiny Expression Number 7 91

    Destiny Expression Number 8 93

    Destiny Expression Number 9 96

Chapter Eight: Personal Year Numbers 1, 2 and 3 100

    Personal Year Number One 100

Personal Year Number Two 103

Personal Year Number Three 105

Chapter Nine: Personal Year Numbers 4, 5 and 6 108

Personal Year Number Four 108

Personal Year Number Five 110

Personal Year Number Six 112

Chapter Ten: Personal Years Numbers 7, 8 and 9 114

Personal Year Number Seven 114

Personal Year Number Eight 116

Personal Year Number Nine 117

Conclusion 118

Index 120

PHOTO REFERENCES 124

REFERENCES 126

Introduction

The unfortunate thing about some people is that they usually have no idea who they really are or what their purpose is in life. Fortunately, numerology is a tool that can help you understand yourself and help you find out what you are born to do.

Some people can be successful in a certain aspect but they are not applying themselves at the right time or at the right environmental conditions. If for instance, someone asks you, "who are you?" We tend to usually give our name or what we do for a living or the kind of achievement, title or position we achieve. However, you have to learn that you

Introduction

are not just your name. Your name is just expressed through you. We're all human beings who are only given a name basically, and we also have a date of birth. The date of your birth has a significant bearing on your life. Once you understand the meaning of the date of your birth for you, you'll be able to know *when* to apply yourself at the right time in a particular way *(how)* to do it so that you can be in a more successful position in life, and perhaps help improve other people's quality of life.

What most numerologists or the people who study this ancient system found out after years of studying and observing individuals and events is that 98% of people are negative or has a negative outlook in life and only 1% is positive. That's pretty staggering right? So what group do you belong into? Obviously, the more you strive to be a part of the 1% the more successful you'll be in any aspect of your life.

Another significant learning of numerologists involves people who make the most money. They found out that there are 9 groups (1 to 9); of all these nine groups, group number 6 seems to make money easily than the rest. You see, the numbers themselves don't really mean anything rather they represent what kind of qualities an individual may have that enables them make the most money. On the

Introduction

other hand, out of the 9 groups, most of the people in group 8 end up in jail – whether they deserve to be there or not as in the case of innocent people who only have been accused of wrongdoings. These are just some of the things that you can do with the system of numerology.

Numerology can help you find out who you are as a human being, where you need to be, what you need to be doing, how you need to do something and when. You can find out significant information about your true identity and purpose through deciphering your name through the system of numerology.

Introduction

Chapter One: Basics of Numerology: Life Path Number, Destiny Expression Number and Personal Year Number

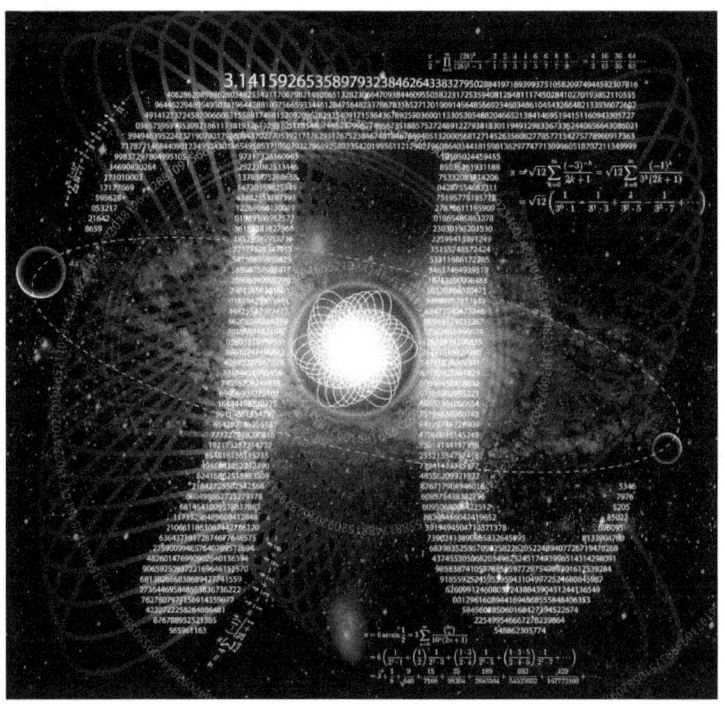

The basics of numerology involve knowing your life path number and your destiny expression number. For beginner's like you this is pretty much all you need to know regarding this ancient system although there are still other methods you can use to further learn the 'truth' about yourself and your life's purpose.

In this chapter, you'll learn the importance and significance of a life path number and your destiny

Chapter One: Basics of Numerology

expression number as well as how to use simple computation to decipher the numerology of the date of your birth and your name. You'll be surprised later on at how this very simple information can coincide to your personality numerology profile and with what you need to do to express it and fulfill your destiny. In the next few sections, you'll also see a few examples of how to compute the date of your birth to get your life path number, and the numbers represented by your name to arrive at your destiny expression number.

In the next few chapters, we will give out the meaning of each life path number and destiny expression number so that you'll have an idea as to what kind of person you truly are – beyond surface – level characteristics, and what you are inclined to do to fulfill your life's mission in this world. Are you excited? Let's get started and add those numbers up! Don't worry this only involves basic math!

Life Path Number

Your life path number is one of the most important and significant number in the art of numerology or in your personality numerology profile. Knowing your life path number will help an individual understand who he/ she really are and the kind of life one will live. It can also help a

Chapter One: Basics of Numerology

person understand one's life path as well as the learning and experiences that an individual set for oneself in this lifetime.

There are 9 life path numbers in numerology. The simplest way of calculating your life path number is by adding the number of your date of birth. Below is a step by step guide example on how you can calculate your life path number. We will use the "Reducing – Down Method":

Important Reminder

Whenever you come upon numbers such as 11, 22 and 33 you should not reduce them down to single – digits because these numbers are known as "Master Numbers." For this example, we will assume that your date of birth is 20th of March 1995 or 20/03/1995.

Step by Step Guideline and Example

Step #1: Since the number 20 is a two – digit number, you should reduce it into a single digit by doing this:

2 + 0

Step #2: The next number is 03 or 3. You don't need to reduce it down since it is a single digit.

Step #3: Reduce down your year of birth by adding it all up like this:

1 + 9 + 9 + 5

Chapter One: Basics of Numerology

Step #4: Now all you need to do is to add it all up and reduce it all down like this:

2 + 0/ 3/ 1 + 9 + 9 + 5

2/ 3/ 24/

2/ 3/ 2+4

2/3/ 6

Reduced Number: 2 + 3 + 6 = 11

Step #5: Since 11 is a Master Number, you don't need to reduce it into a single digit number; therefore, **the life path number for this birth date is 11.**

Below is another example:

Birth date: 05/ 15/ 1983

5/ 1 + 5/ 1 + 9 + 8 + 3

5/ 6/ 21

5/ 6/ 2 + 1

5/ 6/ 3

5 + 6 + 3 = 14

1 + 4 = 5

Life Path Number is 5.

Chapter One: Basics of Numerology

Birth date: 10/ 16/ 1975

1 + 0 / 1 + 6 / 1 + 9 + 7 + 5

1/ 7/ 22

1/ 7/ 2 + 2

1/ 7/ 4

1 + 7 + 4 = 12

1 + 2 = 3

Life Path Number is 3.

Do take note that even if you shortcut the reduce – down method, you'll still get the same answer unless of course your addition is wrong or the birth date of your subject is incorrect. Errors in calculation of your life path number will definitely change the outcome and it will lead you to receiving the wrong interpretation for your personality numerology profile. In the next chapters, you'll get to learn the interpretation of your life path number and how it can also be aligned with your destiny expression number.

Destiny Expression Number

Your destiny expression number is the second most important numerology of your life. The destiny expression number will help you figure out what you need to do, how

Chapter One: Basics of Numerology

you need to do it, and when. If life path number answers the "who" question, the destiny expression number deals with the what, how and when. It will guide you on how you can become the best version of you, it will help you discover your potential, and it may also guide you in fulfilling your purpose in this lifetime. The best part is that your destiny expression number can be used in conjunction with your life path number along with your other significant numerology number in order to see the bigger picture.

You can calculate your destiny expression number using your full name as it appears on your birth certificate. You need to make sure that the spelling is accurate and you must include your second or middle name except other extension names such as Jr., Sr., II, III so forth.

Using the Pythagorean Numerology Chart, you just need to turn your name into its equivalent number before reducing it down. Check out the chart below:

1	2	3	4	5	6	7	8	9
A	B	C	D	E	F	G	H	I
J	K	L	M	N	O	P	Q	R
S	T	U	V	W	X	Q	Z	

Numerology Explained

Chapter One: Basics of Numerology

Step by Step Guideline and Example

Step #1: List down your full name as seen on your birth certificate. Include your middle name and leave out extension names (if any).

For this example we will use the following name:

ASHLEY CLAIRE WEST

Step #2: Convert the name using the chart above

ASHLEY CLAIRE WEST

118357 331995 5512

Step #3: Just like in calculating the life path number earlier, you just need to add up the numbers of the name:

1 + 1 + 8 +3 + 5 + 7 = **25**

3 + 3 + 1 + 9 + 9 + 5 = **30**

5 + 5 + 1 + 2 = **13**

Step #4: As you can see in this example, the total doesn't contain Master Numbers 11, 22 or 33 which is why we will need to turn the total into a single digit and proceed using the reduce – down method:

2 + 5 = **7**

3 + 0 = **3**

1 + 3 = **4**

Chapter One: Basics of Numerology

Step #5: The next step is to add it all up again and reduce it to a single digit if you get a double – digit unless if it is a Master Number (11, 22, 33):

7 + 3 + 4 = 14

1 + 4 = 5.

Destiny Expression Number is 5.

Calculating Your Personal Year Number

To compute for your personal year number, you just need to add up all the digits in your birthday (except the year) and the current year. Here's an example:

Birthday: 20 March 1995

Current Year: 2018

Birth Day + Birth Month + Current Year

2 + 0 + 0 + 3+ 2 + 0 + 1 + 8 = 16 (turn a double digit to a single digit by adding them up)

1 + 6 = 7

Your Personal Year is 7.

Before we delve deeper into the meaning and significance of your life path number and destiny expression number, we just want to remind you that numerology just like other ancient systems should only be taken with a pinch

Chapter One: Basics of Numerology

of salt so to speak because at the end of the day, you are still the master of your own life and destiny. The meanings you will learn in the upcoming chapters will only serve as guide and may also give you an idea on who you are as a being and could give you a clue as to what your life purpose is both the short – term and the long – term.

Chapter One: Basics of Numerology

Chapter Two: Life Path Numbers 1, 2 and 3

In this chapter, we will provide you with the meanings and significance of the first three Life Path Numbers. If you've done the calculation exercise in the last chapter, by now you will have known what your life path number is. Your life path number will give you a clue as to what kind of person you are or what you may need to learn either from your past experiences or present experiences as it will guide you in creating the kind of life you want in alignment to your 'true' self. We will discuss life path numbers 1, 2 and 3 in this chapter. If your life path number is different, you can skip this part for now but it's also best that you read it because you may find it useful especially when you are dealing with people who have these life path numbers.

Chapter Two: Life Path Numbers 1, 2 and 3

Life Path Number 1: The Leader

If your life path number is one, then you are more a 'leader' type of person. The primary purpose of your life is to deal with your sense of confidence and creativity in anything you do. Here's the thing though, since what we're all here to do is usually the 'hardest thing' for us to do, you will experience consistent obstacles in two areas of your life which is

The life path number one is competitive by nature which means you thrive in a competitive kind of environment. The most important thing that leaders like you need to understand is that you must follow your own unique voice. As cliché as it may sound, you need to be the one to lead the pack or march the beat to a different drummer. You are the maestro that guides and leads the whole orchestra because you are creative and innovative, and you need to learn how to turn that into reality because YOU ARE THE ONLY ONE who can do it. You're kind of like Steve Jobs; you are the driving force of innovation in whatever field you choose. Speaking of Jobs, did you know that he also have a one life path number? Well, that says a lot, isn't it?

Your best and highest purpose is to clarify and communicate your unique idea, find the right people and resources to support your idea that can help you manifest your dreams, set it all up, delegate tasks, motivate and

Chapter Two: Life Path Numbers 1, 2 and 3

inspire people through your passion or with humor and just let it run with minimum supervision so that what you've built can one day run without you and you can move on to the next project or if this particular project is really your passion, you can focus on taking it to the next level. That's the type of person you are supposed to be. Now, this might sound boring especially if you've done this a couple of times.

Let's go back and use Steve Jobs again as an example. As you know he's famously known for creating Apple Inc. which took computers and technology to the next level – something that the world has never seen. He placed the power of technology in people's hands and into our pockets which paved the way for the kind of technology and the level of communication we are using today and in the future. He is indeed one of the most brilliant innovators in history and Time Magazine called him as "The Genius Who Changed the World." However, as you may have also seen or heard through various documentaries, interviews and portrayal of him on films and on TV, he also had many struggles – difficult and demanding is an understatement if he was to be described according to his colleagues, business partners, family and friends yet he certainly embodies all the qualities of a one life path.

As a one life path number, you have to understand that life will constantly knock you down but that's the key to the golden castle! One life path number individuals

Chapter Two: Life Path Numbers 1, 2 and 3

understand that this is just how it is for them. And just like other people who are in this category, all you need to do is to face the obstacle head on, embrace it, and understand that all of these challenges need to happen because it is how you'll gain the knowledge, skill level, experience, fortitude, tenacity, discipline and commitment you need to act on the unique or perhaps world – changing ideas of yours.

You see, if everyone can do it, then what's the point right? It's kind of like becoming a boxer versus becoming a teacher; not that one is necessarily better than the other but the expectation of training you'll have to undergo has a huge difference. In this case, you are the boxer. You have to understand and accept that you will have to get beaten up during training because that's what going to make you a better boxer or in the one life path numbers case a leader.

Sometimes you are the one who's ahead of your time as in the case of Steve Jobs; he already saw the future but the technology hasn't catch up yet, or sometimes you're the person who gets beaten down early in life and this could either be your motivation to make a change or it could also bring you down and make you give up your dreams – it's a double edge sword, so to speak.

Here's the thing about life path. Some people are pulled to the opposite direction than what their life purpose indicates for them. It's kind of like Darth Vader; some people "sell their soul to the dark side" just so they can

Chapter Two: Life Path Numbers 1, 2 and 3

fulfill their destiny. It will appear to be the easy route but in the end you'll end up unhappy and miserable because you're not doing what the universe, God, or your higher being called you to do.

If you are a one life path, here are some keywords that may describe who you are:

- You are independent
- You value originality
- You are self – motivated
- You are a high – achiever
- You are very creative
- You are highly competitive
- You are action – oriented

Issues and Struggles of One Life Path Number

Negativity and Lack of Self - Confidence

Since you are all about creativity, independence and achievement, you will often experience fear and paralysis surrounding these issues. You may have severe lack of self – confidence and 'creative block' similar to writers having writer's block where inspirations run dry. Leaders may appear all calm and collected on the outside but on the inside they are struggling with negativity produce by their own ego. You may experience self – doubt and your mind might ponder questions such as "who do you think you are?," you're not good enough," "you don't deserve this or

Chapter Two: Life Path Numbers 1, 2 and 3

that," "you haven't done this thing before, what makes you think you can do it now?" etc.

As a one life path, your job is to ignore those negative messages in your head and not focus on it. You must rip it out completely every time that tape plays in your head because it's like a little devil that will always be there on your shoulder telling you you're not good enough and other lies about you. Try your best not to listen and accept that your failures are not really failures rather they are lessons that move you a step closer to success and fulfillment. Failures are only experiments that could lead you to the next big thing. Focus on this idea and turn negative into a positive. Turn every problem into an opportunity. We also recommend that you read inspiration, motivational or self – help books about how to handle failure, and shift your mind from the negative to a more positive outlook.

Like a boxer, it's imperative for leaders like you to understand that you will need to take a hit and fall down every single time. All you need to do is to keep getting back up, learn the lessons, and try again with relentless self – confidence.

Whenever you're struggling, think about Steve Jobs or other leaders in history, think about the struggles they went through and the monumental challenges they have to overcome both personally and professionally. Sometimes you just really have to take a leap of faith and understand that there will always be the risk of failing.

Addictions

People under the one life path also tend to become addicted to various things such as sex, drugs, smoking, food, alcohol, and even negative thoughts. Make sure to be aware of this tendency and solve it immediately when you see the red flag before it becomes worse.

Constant Flow of Ideas

Leaders are thinkers but it's both a blessing and a curse. What you can do is to overcome overthinking is to find healthy ways to gain clarity and find the time to do something that could help you clear your head such as exercising, engaging in artistic expressions, or travelling so that you won't need alcohol, drugs or other negative habits to slow down and relax your mind.

Aggression

Another struggle that you may face especially when you're not confident or creative is aggression. You may tend to become the most cynical, negative, judgmental and aggressive person in the room. You will tend to lash out at some point especially if your expectations from yourself or

Chapter Two: Life Path Numbers 1, 2 and 3

from other people aren't met. One life path number individuals always want to be number 1 and can also become narcissistic which could be detrimental. So for you to overcome this possible tendencies, you have to constantly be aware of your emotions, communicate it effectively to your team, and lead people to the right path

Choose an equal not a follower

When it comes to choosing a partner both in your personal and professional life, you must choose an equal and not just a mere follower. Leaders sometimes choose someone who is more of a supporter or a follower to them which is why sometimes it's not working. You need to choose an equal both in romance and in business/ career. Some leaders tend to be superior in their personality and they choose partners who are inferior and they wonder why their relationship or marriage is not working.

Neediness

One life path number individuals tend to also be needy especially when they are struggling with self – confidence. They tend to become co – dependent on other people so make sure to watch out for that as well. If you are a one life path, here are some keywords that may describe your 'dark side':

- Self – Absorbed
- Critical
- Competitive
- Angry
- Aggressive
- Cynical
- Narcissist
- Isolated
- Addictive

The ultimate struggle you will face is your lack of self – confidence to act and tap your innate creativeness and innovativeness. In order for you to accomplish your visions and dreams, you have to know that you are here to make a dent in the universe, to leave this world a much better place than you found it. You are a creative force field but you need to make sure that you have clarity, focus, and execution so that you can fulfill your mission. The energy of the one life path number needs to have a tangible life expression and release this energy to benefit the world otherwise you will implode and become self – destructive.

Who You Are:

You are a leader who needs to gain a strong sense of self – confidence in order to act and execute your creative ideas.

Chapter Two: Life Path Numbers 1, 2 and 3

Most Life Path Number 1 is favorable on 21st of July to the 28th of August; 21st of March to the 28th April.

Lucky days for Life Path Number 1 are Monday and Sunday

Fortunate Colors: Shades of Yellow, Gold, Bronze to Golden Brown

Lucky Gems/ Jewels: Amber, Yellow Diamond, Topaz

Notable People in History Born under the Life Path Number 1

- Alexander the Great born on July 1
- U.S. President Garfield born on November 19
- U.S. President Wilson born on December 28
- U.S. President Monroe born on April 28
- U.S. President Hoover born on August 10
- Orville Wright (inventor) born on August 19
- Sven Hedin (explorer) born on February 19
- Chopin (composer) born on March 1
- William Dean Howells (author) born on March 1
- Sir Robert Ball (astronomer) born on July 1
- John Calvin (religious reformer) born on July 10
- Mary Anderson (American actress) born on July 28
- Alexandre Dumas (author) born on July 28
- U.S. President Adams born on Oct 19
- Adelina Patti (Prima Donna) born on February 10
- Edgar Allan Poe (poet) born on January 19

Life Path Number 2: The Mediator

If your life path is number 2, then you are more of a mediator. You are here to learn how to be in harmony with others, how to love and how to have a sense of balance in anything you do. Just like the leader in life path number 1, you will experience consistent obstacles and challenges in your life. You'll learn from the school of hard knocks so to speak. You are the kind of person who thrives whenever you have the chance to serve the needs of a particular group. You are also detail – oriented and action – oriented. There are also lots of two life path number individuals who are quite shy and prefer to be in "behind – the – scenes" rather than in the spotlight. You're the gel that makes it all happen both in your personal and professional life. You are the kind of person that loves to set up win – win situations and can get along with a group.

One of the most important qualities of two life path number individuals is that you are all about love – giving and receiving unconditional love. Needless to say, you have an open and giving heart. However, just like the one life path number, it's also both a blessing and a curse in a way that you are very sensitive and emotional to the point that you may not realized it.

Chapter Two: Life Path Numbers 1, 2 and 3

One of the methods that enable twos to serve a dynamic group successfully is because you know in your heart or through your instinct as to what's going on emotionally with other people. This is your 'innate power' but it can also be exhausting and draining especially if you encounter the so – called "emotional vampires." Emotional vampires are negative people who can suck the life and energy out of you if you aren't aware of it. The key to preventing or overcoming emotional vampires is healthy emotional self – detachment. You have to learn how detach yourself properly from negative people in order to protect yourself and also keep yourself healthy and happy. Individuals who have a life path number two are usually the happiest people around. They are easy to talk to and generally fun to be with. They are always there for everyone and oftentimes focus on keeping other people happy. They have perfected the art of giving and receiving joy and love – this is the true gift of a two.

If you are a two life path, here are some keywords that may describe who you are:

- You are a peacemaker
- You are a harmonizer
- You are a loving person
- You are understanding
- You are detail and action - oriented

- You like to provide service within a group
- You are diplomatic and cooperative
- You are an emotionally sensitive person

Issues and Struggles of Two Life Path Number

Since you're the type of person who is all about harmony, cooperation, balance and love, you will usually experience struggles around these very issues. You are inclined to be combative instead of harmonizing, you tend to be oversensitive and you may look for love in all the wrong places.

The red flag for twos is that they are giving too much of themselves to the point that they will abandon the project they're working on or the person with receding resentment or anger. What you can do is to become aware of this red flag and catch yourself giving too much than what you're supposed to and stop yourself before you implode because the resentment you might experience can be traumatic for you. Like anything else in life, modulation is key. You have to be balanced even in doing something good for a person or an endeavor so that you won't be taken advantage of others and lose yourself in the process.

The inclination to constantly seek outside approval from people is also one of your struggles which is why the

Chapter Two: Life Path Numbers 1, 2 and 3

antidote to that and the lesson you need to learn from this life path number is to seek approval from within rather than from others. Most two life path number people doesn't get recognized for the good that they're doing or isn't given enough credit or acknowledgement for it but here's the thing – you're not meant to be recognized or acknowledge by other people for you to feel fulfilled or happy. So if ever this is an issue you're struggling with, as unfortunate as it may sound, you have to understand that this lifetime is not meant for you to be given credit or acknowledgement even if it could be an obsessive need for you.

As long as you genuinely give yourself for others with a certain amount of balance, you'll be surprised at the rewards or the things that could open up for you.
You may also have issues regarding love because you probably have an unrealistic view of it, you probably give too much of yourself or you probably lose your identity especially if you need to choose a side. Rather than seeing everyone's point of view, you are also inclined to become self – centered especially if you've experienced some sort of emotional wound in your life that it becomes a defense mechanism for you.

If you are a two life path, here are some keywords that may describe your 'dark side':

- You may be overly sensitive
- You may be blunt
- You could be childish
- You tend to need constant approval or acknowledgment
- You sometimes become combative
- You could be an over - giver to the point of resenting it.

Your ultimate struggle is perhaps over – cooperation and withdrawing. Keep in mind that as a mediator, you are meant to create a harmonious atmosphere for both yourself and others, and you're the kind of person who needs to feel that you are an important part of a group or that you are part of something bigger. You feel the most purposeful when you feel that the service you gave either at work or at home has some sort of significance. A two life path number individual needs to express themselves through healthy emotional self – care, love, kindness and selfless service.

Who You Are:

You are a mediator and you're true gift lies in acquiring a strong sense of yourself, balancing your emotional sensitivity and making sure that you have

Chapter Two: Life Path Numbers 1, 2 and 3

personal boundaries so that you'll protect yourself from emotionally negative people.

Most Life Path Number 2 born on the "House of the Moon" are more likely to succeed massively which is from the 20th of June to the 27th of July.
Get along with life path numbers 1 but lesser on 7; or those born on the 7th, 16th or 25th of any month

Lucky days for Life Path Number 2 are Monday, Friday, and Sunday

Fortunate Colors: Shades of Green (light or dark), Cream, and White. As much as possible avoid wearing black, dark red or violet.

Lucky Gems/ Jewels: Moonstones, Jade, Pearls, Pale Green stone

Notable People in History Born under the Life Path Number 2
- Mary Antoinette (Queen of France) born on November 2
- Napoleon III born on April 20
- Ibsen (author) born on March 20
- William Lecky (historian) born on March 20
- King Victor Emmanuel III born on November 11
- Sir Edward Elgar (composer) born on June 2

Chapter Two: Life Path Numbers 1, 2 and 3

- U.S. President Harding born on November 2
- President Poincare (France) born on August 20
- Paul Bourget (author) bon on September 2
- Henry George (author) born on September 2
- Amelia Barr (author) born on March 29
- Max O'Rell (author) born on March 2
- Eugene Field (poet) born on September 2
- Henry George (writer) born on September 2
- Joseph Jefferson (actor) born on February 20
- Pope Leo XIII born on March 2
- Alfred de Musset (poet) born on November 11
- Pope Pius X born on June 2

Life Path Number 3: The Communicator

The purposes of individuals who have are a three life path number is to develop your sense of self – expression and emotional sensitivity in a creative way. You are the type of person who never runs out of ideas. You are generally a performer, an entertainer or perhaps have a sense of wittiness. Three in numerology is the happy number. You love to be around people and you generally have fun socializing. You know how to tell a story and you are creatively expressive. Threes are usually inclined for written or spoken word, and you are also very emotional which is why it's perfect especially if you like to be involved in anything artistic. You are the type of person who can

Chapter Two: Life Path Numbers 1, 2 and 3

absorbed all the information out there and rehash it in your own original way that's relevant and timely before wrapping it all up in a nice package that will be interesting or of help to other people.

If you are a three life path, here are some keywords that may describe who you are:

- You are an upbeat kind of person
- You are cheerful and positive
- You are witty and smart
- You are creative and self – expressive
- You are a natural performer
- You have written or verbal acuity
- You tend to uplift and inspire other people

Issues and Struggles of Three Life Path Number

Since creative self – expression is your major characteristic; you'll mostly experience communication blocks and oversensitivity. Keep in mind that your core issues will usually revolve around the core themes or qualities of your life path number.

For threes, your main issue is self – doubt. This is quite obvious especially for people who are in the creative fields. It becomes a big issue for some people to the point that they develop analysis paralysis and end up talking

Chapter Two: Life Path Numbers 1, 2 and 3

themselves out of a creative endeavor or even in relationships. You are inclined to self – sabotage your own success. The weakness of threes is that they are over – thinkers and not so much of a doer. They are usually the most talented in the room but because of too many ideas in their head sometimes they tend to spread themselves too thin or lose interest on certain things.

Threes are also inclined to struggle with experiencing extreme emotional highs and lows. You are likely to struggle with manic depression due to oversensitivity. As a three life path individual, you need to learn how to master your emotions so that you can express yourself in a creative and authentic way.

Threes usually grew up in a family that has a history of alcoholism, addiction or other family dysfunction that didn't allow the cultivation of having an emotional environment. The antidote to this is to become aware of it and find ways on how you can healthily acknowledge and express your emotions.

Another major struggle for threes particularly when these people haven't embraced their emotional sensitivity is that they are bound to negatively express themselves through bashing, cynicism and being too judgmental.

Chapter Two: Life Path Numbers 1, 2 and 3

Threes are usually the candidate for depression. If you do experience this state every now and then, you need to constantly ask yourself what you truly are depressed about as this will give you a start in dealing with your emotional struggles in a healthy way.

If you are a three life path, here are some keywords that may describe your 'dark side':
- You may experience extreme self – doubt
- You are likely to be moody or depress
- You have extreme emotional lows and highs
- You are afraid of criticism
- You lack follow – through
- You are scattered in your ideas sometimes

Your ultimate challenge is how you can express your feelings and exposing to others your true identity. The antidote to this is knowing that you are born to work with creative expression as well as inspire and communicate to other people.

Who You Are:
You are a communicator and your true gift lies when you acquire a strong inner emotional life, when you learn how to trust your feelings and also use your creativity and talent to uplift and inspire others.

Chapter Two: Life Path Numbers 1, 2 and 3

Most Life Path Number 3 is favorable on period of three such as from February 19 to March 20 to 27; from November 21 to December 20 to 27.

Get along with life path numbers 6 and 9; or those born on the 3rd, 12th, 21st, 30th, 6th, 15th, 24th, 9th, 18th, and 27th of any month

Lucky days for Life Path Number 3 are Tuesday, Thursday, and Friday

Fortunate Colors: Shades of violet and mauve. Secondary colors include rose, blue and crimson

Lucky Gems/ Jewels: Amethyst

Notable People in History Born under the Life Path Number 3

- King George V born on June 3
- Emperor Frederick of Germany born on November 21
- U.S. President Abraham Lincoln born on February 12
- Winston Churchill (British Prime Minister) born on November 30
- Charles Darwin (naturalist) born on February 12
- Sir Alfred Austin (poet) born on May 30
- Richard Cobden (Free Trade) born June 3
- George IV born on August 12
- Pope Benedict born on November 21
- Mark Twain born on November 30

Chapter Two: Life Path Numbers 1, 2 and 3

- Voltaire born on November 21
- William Cullen Bryant (poet) born on November 3
- Ramsay Macdonald (First Labor Prime Minister of England) born on October 12

Chapter Three: Life Path Numbers 4, 5 and 6

This chapter will cover life path numbers 4, 5 and 6.

Life Path Number 4: The Teacher

The primary purpose of your life is to develop a sense of stability, security, and process in anything you do. Just like in previous life path numbers, you will encounter challenges surrounding these traits. You're the type of person who believes in keeping things slow and steady because that's how you will win despite of the fact that it could take years and years of experience and of trials and tribulations. The life path number 4 requires you to not skip the learning process otherwise life is set up in a way for you

Chapter Three: Life Path Numbers 4, 5 and 6

to go back and take the proper steps before you achieve a certain goal.

One of your major strength includes your mastery in building systems as what most teachers have in common. Needless to say, you can make order out of any chaos. You are the kind of person who always wants to keep things in order because that's how you feel a certain sense of control. You're not the kind of person who 'breaks the rules' because you don't want to be seen as unprepared or stupid.
If your life isn't in order and your name calculates to number four, then you need to fix things up so that you can relax and feel safe.

Teachers in general love to learn and can be considered as a student of life. Even if you are not a professional teacher or trainer, you still have that knack of guiding people using your intelligence and organizational ability. Many fours are pet lovers and are also quite creative. You are all about concerted efforts and you are built to employ repeatable processes to guide and teach others. Generally speaking, you love to work hard to get things done.

If you are a four life path, here are some keywords that may describe who you are:

- You are a knowledge seeker

Chapter Three: Life Path Numbers 4, 5 and 6

- You are a master builder of systems
- You are hardworking
- You are reliable
- You strive to follow the rules
- You like to be stable and secure

Issues and Struggles of Four Life Path Number

One of your main struggles is your emotional family wounds. You may have experienced traumatic experiences during your childhood such as growing up with an addictive parent, intense issues with siblings, death of a loved one/s, or being abandoned. What you should do to heal your emotional wounds is to acknowledge and accept all of it because that's part of your purpose in life. Most fours become a caring and emotionally available parent which can be good because this is how you can also heal your emotional wounds in the past by creating a family you wish you had. Even if you decide to not have a family, you can do a correction through caring for your pets, colleagues and other people.

Another issue you may encounter is stubbornness and rigidity that could also extend to your physical body. Many fours have back problems and aren't flexible enough so what you can do to not be someone like a robot who

Chapter Three: Life Path Numbers 4, 5 and 6

strictly follow the rules is to be engaged into some form of activity that can loosen up not just your body but also your rigid mind. At some point, you may also feel overburdened with responsibilities. You tend to get lost in a routine and sometimes you miss lots of opportunities particularly in your finances because you shy away from earning money yet you're the one who needs it to feel safe.

You're the type of person who wants things to be predictable to feel secure. You might feel unhappy with your 9 to 5 job yet you are always afraid and uncomfortable in taking risks. You are linear to the point that you will not take a leap of faith and try something new which can probably make things better for you. If you are a four life path, here are some keywords that may describe your 'dark side':

- You are stubborn
- You are a know – it – all kind of person
- You get lost in routine
- You are rigid
- You have a tendency to repeat mistakes
- You experience family wounds

Your ultimate struggle is that you lack stability, you ignore the process and you feel insecure of yourself. Fours like you are meant to learn, create and build processes using systems. You thrive on stability and security. Your

Chapter Three: Life Path Numbers 4, 5 and 6

main traits are hardwork, endurance and setting up strong foundations.

Who You Are:

You are a teacher and your true gift lies when you accept your emotional family wounds and when you diligently work to achieve your goals and also teach others using the lessons you learned along the way

Most Life Path Number 4 are favorable on June 21 to July 20 – 27; July 22 until the end of August

Get along with life path numbers 1, 2, 7, and 8

Lucky days for Life Path Number 4 are Monday, Saturday, and Sunday

Fortunate Colors: Half – shades; half – tones; electric colors such as blue and grey

Lucky Gems/ Jewels: Sapphire (light/ dark)

Notable People in History Born under the Life Path Number 4

- First U.S. President George Washington born on February 22
- Lord Byron born on January 22

Chapter Three: Life Path Numbers 4, 5 and 6

- Lord Leighton (painter) born on December 4
- Sir Francis Bacon (philosopher) born on January 22
- James Russell Lowell (poet) born on February 22
- Alphonse Daudet (writer) born on May 13
- Sir Arthur Conan Doyle born on May 22
- Julie Hawthorne (author) born on June 22
- Ex – Sultan Abdul Harnid born on September 22
- Saint Augustine born on November 13
- Immanuel Kant (philosopher) born on April 22
- Sir Isaac Pitman (inventor of Shorthand) born on January 4
- Pope Pius IX born on May 13
- Schubert (composer) born on January 31
- Sir Arthur Sullivan (composer) born on May 13

Life Path Number 5: The Freedom Seeker

The primary purpose of your life is to develop a sense of freedom through self – discipline in anything you do. Most five life path number individuals experience various things all at the same time that it's hard for you to filter and prioritize. You are meant to experience the physical world and the zany side of life. You are also a tactile person which means you love to see, taste, or experience things first hand. You are an adventurous type of person and you're all about having fun. Needless to say, you are the life of the party, and you are full of life.

You are here to develop that sense of adventure and fearlessness. If for instance you are a salesperson, you will be lively in selling a product especially if you believe in it. You can reach out to people because you are an agent of change. You are independent and you don't want to be boxed in, so to speak.

You are not the type of person that easily commits to a marriage especially at a young age, you are always looking for the next high or the next big experience, and you don't settle in a relationship. If you ever do settle down, you make a loving and loyal partner but you need to be clear about your personal space. Fives are born to show others how to live a fun, fearless, and adventurous life that is guided through self – discipline.

If you are a five life path, here are some keywords that may describe who you are:

- You are fun and fearless
- You are adventurous and loves to travel
- You like sensual exploration
- You are extremely versatile

Chapter Three: Life Path Numbers 4, 5 and 6

- You are an agent of change
- You have a very high energy towards life in general

Issues and Struggles of Five Life Path Number

The major challenges of a five life path is self – discipline and sense of freedom. You may find yourself working through your fears to come out fine on the other side. You could also be an anti – adventurer because you are fearful of trying new experiences which makes you unhappy since you're getting farther away from your life path.
It becomes hard for you to also maintain self – discipline since you want to experience every single thing. It could be hard for you to maintain a relationship, hold a job, finish school etc. You have a tendency to abandon things because you are constantly seeking for another high.

You are inclined to have dependency swings wherein you either become totally independent to the point of recklessness or dependent to the point where you have so much fear and you think you cannot do things on your own without the help from other people. Since fives are easily seduced by freedom and the idea of a "great escape," they're also the ones who are inclined to struggle with addictions – over - travel, over – party, gambling, sex, alcohol, food, drugs etc. So make sure to watch out for that.

Chapter Three: Life Path Numbers 4, 5 and 6

If you are a five life path, here are some keywords that may describe your 'dark side':

- You get easily bored
- You are inclined to have addictions
- You are paranoid or fearful
- You lack focus and self - discipline
- You are self – centered
- You are drama king/ queen
- You indulge on things

Your ultimate issue is that you don't feel that you have a sense of freedom and adventure or you lack self – discipline. You are here to develop your sense of adventure and freedom using a refined sense of discipline. You thrive whenever you use your lively energy to act upon your sense of freedom.

Who You Are:
You are born to learn on how to moderate your active lifestyle energy and engage in life with fearlessness and fun to show others how they can conquer their fear in their own lives.

Chapter Three: Life Path Numbers 4, 5 and 6

Most Life Path Number 5 are favorable on periods of five from May 21 to June 20 – 27; August 21 to September 20 to 27.

Lucky days for Life Path Number 5 are Wednesday and Friday

Fortunate Colors: light grey and white

Lucky Gems/ Jewels: Diamond, Platinum, and Silver

Notable People in History Born under the Life Path Number 5

- St. Louis of France born on May 23
- H.M King George VI born on December 14
- H. R. H The Duke of Windsor born on June 23
- Shakespeare born on April 23
- Humbert I of Italy born on March 14
- Benedict Arnold (American Spy of the Revolution) born on January 14
- P.T Barnum (circus fame) born on July 5
- Erard (inventor of the Grand Piano) born on April 5
- Fahrenheit (inventor) born on May 14
- Karl Marx (socialist) born on May 5
- Mesmer (Discoverer of Magnetism) born on May 23
- W. T Stead born on February 5

Life Path Number 6: The Nurturer

If your life path number is 6, then you are most likely the nurturer. The primary purpose of your life is to develop your vision in anything you do. You may have experience some struggles in your life or during your earlier years that required you to become responsible. You are sort of a mentor in a way that people often come to you for advice because that's the kind of energy you give off.

The number six relates to family which could mean that you might be someone who starts a family early in your life. And if ever you decide not to settle, you will still have that innate nurturer in you through caring for your parents, friends, colleagues or even pets. Another trait of six life path individuals is that they are a seeker of justice. You value fairness which is why most six are working in judiciary or in the law field. You are also into beautification which is why some six life path individuals work in cosmetic fields, fashion, interior design and other similar occupations.

You are not the kind of person who likes to work for someone else because you don't really take criticism well or you don't want to receive instructions from a superior. You are your own boss and you want to have some sort of control which is why most six people are also entrepreneurs

Chapter Three: Life Path Numbers 4, 5 and 6

or self – employed individuals. You're all about the long – term and you always see the bigger picture because you are innately a visionary.

As a six life path, the lesson you need to learn is a sense of acceptance and patience especially when other people do not see your vision. If you are a six life path, here are some keywords that may describe who you are:

- You are responsible
- You are a visionary
- You are a seeker of justice
- You are an organizer
- You are a connoisseur of beauty
- You are a caretaker

Issues and Struggles of Six Life Path Number

The struggles that you may encounter revolve around acceptance, embracing your vision, and nurturing others. Your main challenge is that you are a perfectionist. You are too idealistic as well to the point that you think whatever you do is the correct way. You hold yourself to very high standards which are why you may encounter instances in your life wherein you've perfected some project but you always see that one tiny thing that doesn't meet your standards and you go nuts. The negative impact to others is that you also expect everyone to meet your high standards

Chapter Three: Life Path Numbers 4, 5 and 6

and if they don't you either let them go or eventually lose them. You also tend to become disappointed in yourself if you don't get it all right. You are very critical of others and often self – righteous due to your perfectionistic trait. You also tend to offend other people's feelings.

If you are a six life path, here are some keywords that may describe your 'dark side':

- You are a perfectionist
- You are too idealistic
- You are very critical of other people
- You have the risk of losing your identity due to unrealistic expectations
- You are always disappointed especially if what you or other people did didn't live up to your high standards.

Your ultimate issue is that you have trouble accepting others and yourself. You tend to also become judgmental of others. Six life path number individuals are here to learn how to accept imperfection while still striving and appreciating perfection of yourself and other people. You thrive when you act on your vision, nurture others, and accept that everything will happen in due time.

Chapter Three: Life Path Numbers 4, 5 and 6

Who You Are:

You are a nurturer and you're true gift is to accept everything as it is without losing yourself, your vision and other people in the process. You are meant to make the world a better place.

Most Life Path Number 6 individuals are favorable on the period of six; April 20 and May 20 to 27; September 21 and October 20 to 27.

Gets along with 3 and 9 with the exception of 5

Lucky days for Life Path Number 6 are Tuesday, Thursday, and Friday.

Fortunate Colors: shades of blue (light to dark), shades of pink or rose. Avoid wearing dark violet and black colors as much as possible.

Lucky Gems/ Jewels: Turquoise and Emeralds

Notable People in History Born under the Life Path Number 6

- Queen Victoria of England born on May 24
- Napoleon I born on August 15
- Frederick the Great born on January 24

Chapter Three: Life Path Numbers 4, 5 and 6

- Joan of Arc born on January 6
- U.S. President Taft born on September 15
- Michael Angelo born on March 6
- Elizabeth Browning (poet) born on March 6
- Henry Ward Beecher (preacher) born on June 24
- President Diaz (Mexico) born on September 15
- Sir William Herschel (astronomer) born on November 15
- Grace Darling (heroine) born on November 24
- Warren Hastings (statesmen) born on December 6
- King George I (Greece) born on December 24
- John Knox (reformer) born on November 24
- Max Muller (philosopher and poet) born on December 6
- Count de Paris (Louis Philippe) born on August 24
- Admiral Peary (North Pole explorer) born on May 6
- Rembrandt (painter) born on July 15
- George Westinghouse (inventor) born on October 6

Chapter Three: Life Path Numbers 4, 5 and 6

Chapter Four: Life Path Numbers 7, 8 and 9

This chapter will cover life path numbers 7, 8 and 9.

Life Path Number 7: The Seeker

If your life path is number 7, you can be compared to a seeker. The primary purpose of your life is to develop your sense of openness and trust in anything you do. As you may know or have heard, the number 7 in both numerology and in religious aspect is related to spirituality. You are meant to have an internal journey while you're here on earth. You are all about developing your personal connection to a higher

Chapter Four: Life Path Numbers 7, 8 and 9

being whether you call it God, Universe, or in Star Wars – The Force.

The contrast with people who are 7 life path is that you are also an analytical person. You thrive in constantly seeking knowledge and the truth about life in general just like a philosopher but on the other hand, you are also very intuitive which can be hard at times if you haven't learn yet on how to integrate your analytical and skeptical brain with your intuition. What usually happens is that you shut down your analytical brain and only listen to your intuition, or vice – versa.

The lesson you need to learn is for you to know how to seamlessly integrate your analytical brain and your psychic abilities. One way of doing this is through taking time to know yourself better. You are the kind of person who digs deep about how you think and feel about virtually everything. Another way is through connecting with nature; you're the one who loves the outdoors and you may find a body of water relaxing. Needless to say, you feel more connected with yourself by spending time in nature or have sometime for isolation.

There would be instances in your life where you just don't feel you belong in this world or in this lifetime. You may also have trouble sleeping since your mind is highly active which is why meditation is needed to quiet your brain. You may also feel that you are an outside observer like a spy.

The task of seven life path is to hone your analytical brain as well as your intuitive ability. When you successfully learn how to integrate this two aspects of yours, that's when you will find out your true gift in this lifetime. Combining your analysis and intuition will result to you having intelligence and wisdom. Your task is also developing your trust both in yourself, in others, and in the Universe. You need to also develop openness and learn to engage with people. If you are a seven life path, here are some keywords that may describe who you are:

- You are highly intuitive
- You always ask "why" on everything
- You are analysis driven
- You need time alone and in nature
- You have a highly refined mind
- You are an 'old soul'

Issues and Struggles of Seven Life Path Number

Chapter Four: Life Path Numbers 7, 8 and 9

Sevens have trust issues. You may oftentimes feel betrayed both by others and by yourself. It's hard for you to trust someone and because of that others may also think that you aren't trustworthy. When it comes to relationships, you're the type of person who wants to be in a relationship but you also don't. There will be times that you find yourself attracting people into your life that are dishonest, not open and not trustworthy, and then you go "I knew it, they're all like that."

Once you find the right person to be with, and you commit yourself to working through your trust issues and you open yourself up to vulnerability, you tend to become the most loyal partner. If you haven't found your spiritual base yet you may feel like a 'lost soul,' this is why it's important that you believe in a certain higher power or higher being otherwise you can become a superficial person. You are also inclined to struggle with addictions that detour you in finding the answers to your life questions or your life purpose. You are also inclined to always be frustrated especially if you are resisting the flow of life; you tend to think that no one is doing anything about this or that etc. You are also inclined to be depressed because of your internal journey. This is because you are bound to do some soul searching which is why you have to welcome emotional ups and downs into your life because that's how you'll find

Chapter Four: Life Path Numbers 7, 8 and 9

who you truly are. Needless to say, the obstacles that you will face in your life will serve as the foundation of the wisdom you need to learn and use it to teach other seekers.

If you are a seven life path, here are some keywords that may describe your 'dark side':

- You have a sharp tongue
- You are inclined to be depressed and frustrated
- You can become superficial
- You may feel lost and betrayed
  You may struggle with addiction

Your ultimate issue is trust in yourself and others as well as being open and vulnerable. You thrive when you use your brain along with your heart or soul. You need to develop your ability to align yourself with your intuition to answer the hardest questions of life.

Who You Are:

You are a seeker and your true gift is to cultivate a sense of inner peace through seeking your truth and sharing your wisdom to others and with the world.
Most Life Path Number 7 individuals are favorable on the period of seven from June 1 to July 20 to 27.

Chapter Four: Life Path Numbers 7, 8 and 9

Gets along with number 2 or Master 11

Lucky days for Life Path Number 7 are Monday and Sunday (same with life path number 2)

Fortunate Colors: shades of green, yellow and white. As much as possible, avoid weary very dark colors.

Lucky Gems/ Jewels: moonstones, pearls, "cat's – eyes," moss agate

Notable People in History Born under the Life Path Number 7

- Queen Elizabeth born September 7
- Empress Charlotte of Mexico born on June 7
- Charles Dickens born on February 7
- Oscar Wilde born on October 16
- Ernst Haeckel (naturalist) born on February 16
- Camille Flammarion (astronomer) born on February 25
- Prince Imperial (Napoleon) born on March 16
- Ralph Waldo Emerson (poet) born on June 25
- Andrew Carnegie born on November 25
- Sir Isaac Newton (astronomer) born on December 25
- Rousseau (French poet) born on April 16

Chapter Four: Life Path Numbers 7, 8 and 9

Life Path Number 8: The Powerhouse

You are the type of person that pretty much does it all; you are financially abundant and you are also balance in terms of control and power in anything you do. The number 8 in numerology is the money number, and people in this group usually share a relentless characteristic.

You want to get a handle of your sense of personal power and this is where life will constantly challenge you. Once you get a grasp of personal power, you are then ready to take it to next level money – wise. You are a resilient type of person and financially speaking, you're the type of person who can make tons of money, go bankrupt and make it all of it back again and maybe more. Making a fortune is quite easy for you despite of the rise and fall.

Most 8 life path number are best suited for execute level positions such as a CEO, entrepreneur, business or industry mogul etc. because they also tend to be directive and have a sense of being in charge. Lots of people tend to look up to you and you're also the kind of person that sort of embodies the cliché "it's not what you know, it's who you know" because you love referring people to other people. You are also a very opinionated individual and have a strong sense of will. You are outspoken and loves to connect with people.

Chapter Four: Life Path Numbers 7, 8 and 9

One of your primary objectives on earth is to develop your relationship with abundance specifically in the area of finance, authority, control and power.

If you are an eight life path, here are some keywords that may describe who you are:

- You like to make money
- You are all about abundance
- You want control or authority
- You are the pillar of community
- You are an influencer

Issues and Struggles of Eight Life Path Number

Your main issues will revolve about money (gaining, losing or inheriting it). You are called to learn about the power of money, about how to use it properly, how to help others using money and the ethics involve in making it. You may also get into conflict with family members regarding money issues, you are inclined to become greedy or a hoarder of money for the sake of it.

There are also 8 life path that struggle with making a fortune and can even get into poverty. Some eights think that money is the root of all evil while others only settle for wishful thinking never making any.

Chapter Four: Life Path Numbers 7, 8 and 9

Your major red flag is being over – focused on making money which can lead to various family issues, greediness or on the opposite, you may tend to always lose money if you don't know how to control the love or hate for money. If you are an eight life path, here are some keywords that may describe your 'dark side':

- You are over – focused on money
- You can be aggressively outspoken
- You are highly opinionated
- You are inclined to be greedy
- You tend to become a workaholic
- You struggle with family wounds and ethics

Your ultimate struggle is your love - hate relationship with money, power as well as abundance. You thrive whenever you are thinking big, creating a fortune, having an abundant mindset and being balance in your sense of control both in your life and in the world.

Who You Are:

You are a powerhouse! You have the ability to experience creating wealth and using it to build lasting value and connect with your sense of personal control while showing other people to do the same. You are meant to show others how to create a fortune and not lose yourself in the process.

Most Life Path Number 8 individuals are favorable on the period of eight from December 21 to January 20 to 27; February 19 to 26.

Lucky days for Life Path Number 8 are Monday, Saturday and Sunday

Fortunate Colors: shades of black, purple, dark blue and dark grey

Lucky Gems/ Jewels: Amethyst, Black Pearl, Dark – stoned Sapphire, Black Diamond

Notable People in History Born under the Life Path Number 8

- Mary I of England (Bloody Queen Mary) born on February 17
- Joseph Chamberlain born on July 8
- George Bernard Shaw born on July 26
- U.S. Admiral Dewey born on Dec 26
- Jenner (discovered vaccinations) born on May 17
- La Fontaine born on July 8
- Sir John Millais (painter) born on June 8
- Pierpont – Morgan (Financier) born on April 17
- J. D. Rockefeller born on July 8
- Jules Verne (novelist) born on February 8
- John Wesley (preacher) born on June 17
- Sir Humphrey Davey born on December 17

- Alfonso XIII of Spain born on May 17
- Prince Albert (consort of Queen Victoria) born on August 26
- Colonel Cody (Buffalo Bill) born on February 26
- Louis Conde of France born on September 8
- Gounod (composer) born on June 17

Life Path Number 9: The Humanitarian

You are the kind of person that acts upon your sense of integrity and also cultivate a deep sense of wisdom in anything you do. In numerology and in many ancient systems, the number nine is known as the number of completion. You are sort of an old soul so to speak. You are perhaps required to master the elements of your number as well as the qualities of other numbers.

This number is not just about completion but also about letting go. You may probably experience lots of losses in your life not just in relationships but also in your career, finances, health etc. However, this is an opportunity for you to master letting things go without resistance but rather with acceptance, wisdom and grace. You may seem to also defend the 'underdog' or you could be that person. You thrive when you are serving for the greater good since you have a giving heart as with most humanitarians of this world. You are also quite charismatic and have a way of connecting to people.

Chapter Four: Life Path Numbers 7, 8 and 9

You are also a natural teacher, healer and leader which is why most people around you think that you know what you're doing even when you don't because you give off that reliable appeal.

Most nines are philanthropists, entrepreneurs, social workers, artists and the likes as long as you feel that you are contributing to something for a bigger purpose or for the greater good. You are very creative and a hopeless romantic! What you're here to learn is to develop and cultivating your sense of integrity and wisdom in every aspect of your life. If you are a nine life path, here are some keywords that may describe who you are:

- You are an old soul
- You have a big heart and a giver
- You are charismatic and dynamic
- You are romantic and also idealistic
- You may have experience many losses to learn the "art of letting go"
- You are all about being complete as a human being

Issues and Struggles of Nine Life Path Number

Integrity and wisdom are your values and/ or things you need to learn but just like in other life path numbers, it's

Chapter Four: Life Path Numbers 7, 8 and 9

also where you will get to experience some form of issues and hindrances. Nine life paths are inclined to sort of become a "rebel without a cause" wherein you could be influencing people to some things for no reasonable cause. This tendency could partly be because life is constantly testing you to learn how to let go of things that you can't control, and allow yourself to be transformed and change in different aspects of your life. It's hard for nine life path individuals to accept change with an open heart which is why that's what you needed to work on. You need to learn how to move forward without resistance otherwise you will experience resentment whenever you look back.

You are being called to live in the present instead of constantly holding on or looking back in the past because the past wouldn't serve you in anyway and could only create bitterness in your heart.

You may also be caught up in sort of a family issue wherein you will have to strive for your own dreams just to have your own identity because most nines are highly linked to what their parents or grandparents etc. have done and you are sort of expected to do the same (i.e. family business, professions, etc.) which could be hard. If that's not the case for you, sometimes nine life path still experience family – related issues in sort of a similar degree like for instance,

Chapter Four: Life Path Numbers 7, 8 and 9

getting caught up in your parent's messy divorce, you are adopted or other situations that requires you to let go of the past in order to redefine your true identity.

Other people always think that you're in control of everything and that you're always fine even when you're not, and so you have to do recognize that there's nothing wrong with asking for help and support from other people especially when you need it the most. If you are a nine life path, here are some keywords that may describe your 'dark side':

- It could be hard for you to let go
- You may struggle with bitterness and despair
- You may be enmeshed with family dynamics
- It's hard for you to ask for help
- You could have issues with honesty and manipulation

Your ultimate struggle is being consistent with your sense of integrity as well as letting go of past issues. Your goal as nine life path individual is to help humanity by using your creativity and talent while at the same time cultivating a sense of wisdom and integrity. It's your calling to serve people and serve a higher cause

Who You Are:
You are a humanitarian and you're primary purpose is to not resist life as it flows in you. You are called to appreciate the present, be in the 'now' and also learn to let go while using the lessons you learned from past experiences so that you don't only help yourself but also others.

Most Life Path Number 9 individuals are favorable on the period of nine; March 21 to April 19 to 26; October 21 to November 20 to 27.

Gets along with numbers 3, 6, 7

Lucky days for Life Path Number 9 are Tuesday, Thursday and Friday

Fortunate Colors: shades of red and crimson; pink and rose tones

Lucky Gems/ Jewels: Bloodstone, Garnet and Ruby

Notable People in History Born under the Life Path Number 9
- U.S. President Theodor Roosevelt born on October 7
- U. S. President Grover Cleveland born on March 18
- Lord Carson (Irish Leader) born on February 9
- Sam Gompers (Labor Leader, USA) born on January 27

Chapter Four: Life Path Numbers 7, 8 and 9

- President Ulysses Grant born on April 27
- Sir James Barrie (author) born on May 9
- Julia Ward Howe born on May 27
- Ernest Renan (author) born on February 27
- Jay Gould (financier) born on May 27
- Elizabeth, Empress of Austria born on August 18
- Kepler (astronomer) born on December 27
- Louis Kossuth (Hungarian Patriot) born on April 27
- Paganini (violinist) born on February 18

  George Stephenson (inventor of Steam Engine) born on June 9

Chapter Five: Master Numbers 11, 22 and 33

In numerology, master numbers 11, 22 and 33 are heightened expressions or qualities of numbers 2, 4 and 6 respectively.

Master Number 11

Master 11 is very similar to the life path number two but you have added qualities and on the flipside more intense challenges. Your primary purpose is to develop your sense of intuition, healing and creativity for the greater good which you can do in various ways such as artistic endeavors, or working with different healing modalities. Most eleven life path individuals end up being a writer, teacher, entertainer, and healer.

The master number 11 also denotes that you are a double 1 which means that you have the quality of being a leader and you exhibit confidence yet it also denotes that you are a 2 (1 + 1) which is all about love and harmony. This is the reason why the challenges you may have or will face in your lifetime is quite unique and a combination of the number one and two life path numbers.

You are also a natural healer; by that I mean that you have "healing powers" just by your mere presence. Isn't it cool? You don't literally have to do anything because your presence is already enough to heal somebody or perhaps make somebody feel better. You may encounter people telling you that you have that calming presence or you evoke that good feeling vibe whenever you're in the room; take this to heart because that is part of what you're called to do. Keep in mind that you are enough just as you are – that's how powerful your life path number is. So, ignore those thoughts in your head about you not being good enough or something because you already are. As a matter of fact, you are more than enough!

This calming or healing quality of yours also extends to your creative ambitions and endeavors. You can touch

Chapter Five: Master Numbers 11, 22 and 33

people's lives with your artistic or creative work just like a painting in an exhibit that you just look at yet already has evoke some profound meaning to the viewer. Your energy can create an impact to people's lives through the work that you do.

Some of the challenges that you'll encounter could be you'll feel as if whatever you do is not enough. You may also be uncomfortable in getting the spotlight because you're happy working behind – the – scenes just like a two life path yet the Master 11 pushes you to take center stage. You are not accepting of criticism which is why it's your responsibility to learn how to protect yourself from outside forces emotionally and mentally because you are not comfortable in handling criticisms which you will definitely encounter if you're the one on the spotlight.

You will also constantly be in battle with self – doubt because this master number is designed to set you up in battling your quite forceful ego. You will feel like you are going back and forth with feelings of being superior and inferior.

The master 11 life path number urges you to take inspired leadership but you may oftentimes feel as if you're constantly leaping from rings of fire, one after another just to achieve your goals.

Chapter Five: Master Numbers 11, 22 and 33

This life path also prepares you and lets you experience various challenges that will enable you to learn about life and embrace your high level of intuition and spirituals while acting upon your creative gifts and abilities to bless the world.

Most elevens have an online presence and they are also fond of using the word "love." You are emotionally sensitive and highly intuitive which can sometimes be a blessing and a curse. What you need to do is to use your inner psychic ability to protect yourself emotionally especially if you're with negative people or those emotional vampires otherwise they will drain you and prevent you from achieving your mission in life.

Your real power comes whenever you are doing any creative or artistic pursuit. You are very intuitive and you give off that healing energy both through your creative work or you are in the field of healing.
Your main purpose in life and your main calling is to heal and transform other through your creativity and selfless service.

Chapter Five: Master Numbers 11, 22 and 33

Master Number 22

Master 22 is very similar to the life path number four but you have added qualities and on the flipside more intense challenges. Your primary purpose is to develop your building and organizing ability through creating projects that would be beneficial to a wide arena of humankind. Just like other master numbers, you are called in this spiritual path that will push you out of that "slow and steady" quality of the life path number four which can again be uncomfortable for you though you'll eventually get used to it. It is definitely contrary to the life path number four as this one will prod you to sort of coming out of your predictable, secured, "follow – the – rules" way of living. The number two is also about being in harmony and love, but you have to combine that with a four which is all about process and stability which is why the challenges you will encounter are also quite unique.

As a master number 22 life path individual, you are called to use the step – by – step qualities of the life path number four while aligning it with a higher level of action and purpose. You are called to take risks from time to time so as to not be too stable and secured, and this could be hard for you especially when stakes are high.
You are a master builder, and your mission involves creating a solid foundation while also looking at the bigger picture.

Chapter Five: Master Numbers 11, 22 and 33

Your true gift lies in the fact that you are a system builder but this also entails some struggles because you may from time to time feel as if you're not up for the task or you're not entitled to success. This master number can cause you to become wealthy or even famous but since you have the qualities of a life path number four, you may cringe to the idea of abundance which can be mentally dragging for most people who aren't dreaming of having so much just liked many fours.

This life path will also push your spiritual practices down to the material world. Perhaps the best example is Oprah Winfrey. She's famous, wealthy, and also now known as a spiritual teacher since her life path number is also a master number. If you really think about it, she could just be a teacher for a small group but she took it up to the next level by being a master teacher to everyone around the world. She is now helping millions of people change their lives for the better through her seminars, podcasts, books, her OWN network, and other spiritual – teaching related endeavors to reach and teach about life.

Oprah aligned herself and live up to the energy of the master number 22 and this kind of happiness and success can also come upon you or anyone who are up for the challenge. Speaking of challenges, you must try to avoid being too stubborn because most twenty – twos are inclined to have that "know – it – all" attitude which is a heightened level of the energy of the number four. What you need to do to overcome this challenge is delegation. You need to learn how to delegate tasks and hand over responsibilities after you build a system for other people so that you can also focus on your own tasks otherwise you may experience a burnout and not get anything done at all. Realize that you need help and learn how to surrender and trust that the right people will come to help you fulfill your mission so that you can serve the greater good.

You thrive whenever you embrace your higher sense of wisdom and act upon it to fulfill your purpose. You as a master builder and teacher are called to change the lives of many people on a practical level. You are also called to manifest your ideas and turn it into practical ways that people can use in their day to day lives. You need to learn how to dream big, and also ask yourself what is your true passion in life and pursue that certain field.

Master Number 33

Master 33 is very similar to the life path number six but you have added qualities and on the flipside more intense challenges. Your primary purpose is to develop your sense of being an inspired visionary and also a master healer. And just like the other master numbers, this is a

Chapter Five: Master Numbers 11, 22 and 33

spiritual path that calls you to tap into one's creative mind as well as your emotions. You are also called to act upon your nurturing presence since you are a double three which means you're inclined to express yourself creatively and you are also emotionally sensitive. At the same time, you are also a six which means you have than visionary, nurturing and accepting qualities.

Just like master numbers 11 and 22, you are set up to encounter unique challenges in order to fulfill your purpose in life. Your primary mission in life is to bring about healing and bring forth a higher form of love. Being a double three means you have to accomplish your mission with a sense of fun, joy and genuineness.

Most thirty – threes are wives, doctors, police, philanthropists or simply people who work behind – the – scenes; just like other master numbers, it can manifest in whatever form of life conditions. You are called to teach and show the power of love through your own life. You serve as a conduit of healing in whatever form you engage in. This life path number calls you to be in leadership positions and compels you to have visionary goals with a genuine heart. You're the kind of person that goes to say hospice facilities or anything of the similar degree because you give off that kind of comfort energy and can naturally bring solace to people.

Chapter Five: Master Numbers 11, 22 and 33

There are plenty of ways that you can live up to your master number by aligning yourself with the energy of the 33. You are also more focused on giving otherwise you are not aligned with your true mission in life.

One of the challenges you will face is that feeling of being over – burdened and could take a hit on your emotional aspect because you may sometimes feel that you're taking on the wounds of the world even though you're on the path of healing and helping people.

The number 33 is perhaps the most challenging master number among the three because you can easily veer off track quite easily if you don't know how to focus. Another flipside includes becoming extremely self – righteous or self – absorbed which can pave the way for struggling with addictions and other bad behaviors if you don't know how to channel this energy in a constructive kind of way. You can easily sabotage yourself and also suffer from too much paranoia.

If you manage to align yourself with the energy of the master number 33, then you are bound for greatness. Meryl Streep is a master number 33 and so are other famous personalities that influenced our world through their amazing energy.

You are an inspired visionary and a master healer, and you thrive best when you are nurturing and healing on

Chapter Five: Master Numbers 11, 22 and 33

either a personal level or on a grand scale. This life path number comes with many challenges and struggles which means that you have to make sure that your feet is on the ground so as not to get disappointed when the world doesn't meet your high level of standards and expectations. The master number 33 is calling you to act upon your heart – centered vision for humanity.

Chapter Six: Destiny Expression Numbers 1, 2, 3 and 4

This chapter will cover destiny expression numbers 1, 2, 3, and 4.

Destiny Expression Number 1

In numerology, this destiny number denotes that you must become the #1 on anything you set out to do in your life. You must find your own voice and develop your leadership abilities so that you can succeed in achieving your dreams, goals or in whatever passion you pursue.

Chapter Six: Destiny Expression Numbers 1, 2, 3 and 4

The destiny expression number one calls you to have a sense of individuality and develop independence. You must learn how to tap into your inner power so that you can achieve things in your life. Your destiny is to become the best in everything you do which means you have very high standards for yourself, and you expect others to do the same – which can start some conflicts and challenges because obviously not everyone can always live up to your expectations, and you may end up disappointed or frustrated so try to balance it out.

The purpose of this destiny number of yours is for you to initiate the lead which means you need to develop your ability to be courageous, learn on being independent and responsible especially with your unique ideas, and also develop self – confidence to execute.
Just like many leaders in history, the way to achieve what you are destined to do is to fail forward. Expect that your life will be full of challenges that you need to overcome but this is because it's how you're going to be more innovative and can help you in implementing your ideas.

A one destiny expression number will prepare you to develop your self – confidence despite your failures along the way. You will encounter lots of failures, of trials and tribulations but this is what you need to strengthen yourself and your mind. You must learn to keep trying again and

Chapter Six: Destiny Expression Numbers 1, 2, 3 and 4

keep learning from your failures as this will bring about your ultimate success. You will also encounter lots of naysayers or people who may doubt you and not believe in your ideas which can be an opportunity for you to practice your determination and willpower. You shouldn't let other people's criticisms stop you from achieving your vision. You must learn to push through with gusto as you are not meant to follow the crowd.

The destiny expression number one insists that you are the one in charge and you must be decisive even if you are challenge with holding yourself back or lacking confidence. You must establish the attitude of being independent, of having your own decisions and following it through. You are original, creative, responsible, and meant to become a leader in whatever path you will pursue in alignment with your life path number.

Destiny Expression Number 2

In numerology, this destiny number denotes that you are destined to gather people together to create that sense of love, peace, diplomacy and harmonious relationship or atmosphere. Your primary purpose is to be a proponent of balance, cooperation, harmony and love in anything you do. For you, love is the pillar of your life which also means that finding the right relationship (romantic or otherwise) is very

Chapter Six: Destiny Expression Numbers 1, 2, 3 and 4

important for you. You are all about relationships, and you are here to learn how you can properly relate to yourself and to other people.

This destiny expression number sets you up for a path of being diplomatic and having patience which means that you are called to seek to serve a higher purpose for the greater good whether it is in your family, business, friends, social groups etc. You are also here to care for others, to open your heart out, and also learn how to adapt and focus. This destiny expression number demands you to go out and socialize to people otherwise isolation will make you pessimistic towards life, and you will be prone to depressive feelings as well as inaction. You are at your best whenever you are helping other people and contributing for something whether in a small group or in a grand scale.

You are also somewhat oversensitive which can make you confrontational instead of being a peacemaker. A red flag for you is needing incessant reinforcement from other people because you will just disappointed since that's not how life is set up for you. Even if you find yourself being aggressive, indecisive, passive or lacking focus you are ought to become a harmonizer and create a peaceful atmosphere in whatever you pursue.

Chapter Six: Destiny Expression Numbers 1, 2, 3 and 4

You are a very sensitive yet highly intuitive person but it's both a blessing and a curse. Your job is to learn how to acknowledge and encourage yourself despite of negative influences of other people to prevent yourself from seeking validation through what other people think about you or doing what they expect you to do.

As harsh and unfortunate as it may sound, your life is set up to be in – between conflicting situations because that's how you can learn how to use your mediation abilities and diplomatic skills. It is indeed ironic since you're the kind of person who as much as possible doesn't want to be involved in any conflict or you simply want to be peaceful. This is why it's up to you on how you will set up personal boundaries and protect yourself emotionally in order to live up to your destiny.

Destiny Expression Number 3

In numerology, this destiny number denotes that you are destined to communicate, inspire, and express yourself. You are also destined to uplift other people. This destiny expression number primarily calls you to heal and energize humanity through your communicative and performance abilities as well as through your self – expression. The primary purpose of your life is to develop that sense of positivity, compassion, happiness and enthusiasm. You are

Chapter Six: Destiny Expression Numbers 1, 2, 3 and 4

an eccentric kind of person and you are a source of joy for others. You inspire people through your authentic self – expression. If you don't use your talents and skills creatively, you will feel unhappy and may also go through depression or worse go off the tracks and find yourself in destructive behaviors. This is why it's important for you to pursue your life calling through focus, belief and embrace the challenges along the way.

The number three usually brings with it so many talents that could be hard for you to focus on just one which is why you are bound to procrastinate or perhaps encounter hurdles that's hard to overcome. You will also be challenge to identify your emotional aspect. Your gift of words – both oral and written – can also be a way of serving others. You are light – hearted, easy to talk to, have a sense of humor, and also a good listener.

Some of the challenges you'll encounter involves your emotional life which means you are inclined to depression, over - analysis, and become judgmental. You may find it uncomfortable whenever you are speaking in front of a crowd, and that's most likely because of your past wounds during your childhood years. What you can do is to accept the past and acknowledge your feelings as doing this can help you gain clarity and wisdom. This destiny number calls you to express yourself truthfully so that you can inspire others to do the same.

Destiny Expression Number 4

In numerology, this destiny number denotes that you are destined to create something of value so that people around you or even those whom you don't know can benefit and practically apply it to their daily life. You are inclined to build something of lasting value like a business, an organization or even a family. You're all about building security and stability. You are reliable, hardworking, a cornerstone in the community and you are also someone whom people can trust easily. And because of these qualities, you have the potential to establish a great and lasting marriage, career, or company. You are also a systems builder which means you are an organized person.
Some of your challenges and struggles include being rigid and stubborn. You have a tendency to avoid hardwork, you may shy away from starting a family, or you are inclined to avoid building lasting things.

The destiny expression number four calls you to find work that will make you feel alive that will satisfy your sense of purpose and value. On the flipside though, it may be hard for you to find a career that would ultimately satisfy

Chapter Six: Destiny Expression Numbers 1, 2, 3 and 4

you but when you do find the path for you, this is where you will be at your best and where you will joyfully thrive.

One of the struggles you may encounter is perfectionism and high standards to the point that you become self – sacrificing. You want to have control in everything you do and delegation may be hard for you. Others may find it hard to please because they fail to meet your expectations even if your intentions and perfectionism is for the greater good. Another struggle you may encounter is that you don't want to feel or look stupid. You may also be disappointed if someone failed to inform you on something. You are also afraid to take risks, which is why some destiny expression fours wake up one day when it's already too late and realized that none of their dreams or goals came true. It may be hard for you to step outside of your own box that you set up or imposed for yourself. This is why you must learn how to take calculated risks.

Even if this destiny expression number sets you up on the path of organizing, managing or establishing a solid foundation, you must learn how to take criticisms in a constructive way, and you must also learn how to be patient because as the saying goes, great things take time. What you should do to achieve success is to make sure that your goals are clear to you, plan it out and follow a step – by – step procedure and just keep doing what you need to do until

Chapter Six: Destiny Expression Numbers 1, 2, 3 and 4

your dreams are manifested in the real world. Never let hindrances get in the way of achieving your vision and understand that it will take effort and endurance before you reach your goals in life.

Chapter Six: Destiny Expression Numbers 1, 2, 3 and 4

Chapter Seven: Destiny Expression Numbers 5, 6, 7, 8 and 9

This chapter will cover destiny expression numbers 5, 6, 7, 8 and 9.

Destiny Expression Number 5

In numerology, this destiny number denotes that you are destined to create change and influence people through your own example on how to live life to the fullest. This destiny expression number call you to be flexible, adapting to change, sense of freedom and opens you up for life's greatest adventure. The guiding force in your life is freedom.

Chapter Seven: Destiny Expression Numbers 5, 6, 7, 8 and 9

You are at your best whenever you experience things first – hand, and your main goal is to develop this freedom along with self – discipline and use it to create something constructive.

This destiny expression number also urges you to welcome risks and be more courageous as these will help you explore the world, follow your curiosity and share your awesome energy to others. Most destiny fives are wise, philosophical, and has a spiritual mindset. You may compare your life path as something like a rollercoaster wherein there is always full of surprises, of ups and downs, and mind – blowing experiences at every turn. You are all about liberating yourself from the societal dogma and you aren't afraid to try new things.

One of your struggles is paranoia, analysis paralysis, fearfulness and self – absorption. Other people may also find you baffling even if you don't have any intention to do so and you're just simply following your own instincts. You may encounter problems with your relationships because of your heightened self – centered emotion wherein your family, friends, or relatives may feel exasperated in some way.

Since you are all about freedom, one of your challenges is not having enough freedom. This means that

Chapter Seven: Destiny Expression Numbers 5, 6, 7, 8 and 9

you will encounter plenty of restrictions and hindrances along the way in some aspects of your life; you should consider it as an opportunity because it will help you practice your sense of freedom with self – discipline to get through the restrictions that you may face.

My advice to you is to learn how re – calibrate yourself and be optimistic even to change because this is how you're going to fulfill your purpose and inspire people how to be more courageous through your own life experiences.

You must also keep in mind that you learn how to practice self – control and discipline yourself through setting up boundaries so that you won't go off tracks in your life path. You must clearly understand the line that separates freedom and irresponsibility or recklessness otherwise your life will become chaotic. The number five destiny expression also spells trouble through excessiveness so it's your job to control and balance it.

Destiny Expression Number 6

In numerology, this destiny number calls you to provide a safe nest not only for yourself but also for your loved ones. You are destined to learn about taking

Chapter Seven: Destiny Expression Numbers 5, 6, 7, 8 and 9

responsibility and service whether it's within your business, workplace, community, friends or family. Your true gift lies in creating balance, love and harmony. You have to also learn how about acceptance as this is very important in the life path that the destiny expression number six has set out for you. You sort of give out that prim and proper appearance with an authoritative aura.

You are also about damage control but in a negative sort of way. For instance, if things are all going according to plan, you tend to start some kind of issue so that you can have something to focus on. What you need to learn is to take the time to celebrate success or just be happy and have an accepting attitude when things are all going your way so that you can avoid paranoia.

The destiny expression number six also sets you up in a way that you will develop further your sense of responsibility which is why you may have already encounter trials and tribulations in your early years.
You tend to become a people – pleaser which can become a problem if you don't draw the line. You are also inclined to think that others always need you and also kind of resenting that people always count on you. Make sure to watch out for people who are more of a patient than a partner otherwise

Chapter Seven: Destiny Expression Numbers 5, 6, 7, 8 and 9

you may find yourself as someone who is more of an enabler and not a nurturer which is supposedly your life path.

You must learn how to balance being responsible in a certain way and not to the point that you will have to do everything yourself or you become someone who has set very high expectations and have that perfectionist attitude. On the other hand, you don't also want to become over – the – top irresponsible, controlling, judgmental and self – centered. Make sure you strike the right balance in terms of your sense of being a responsible individual, and of course learn to delegate and trust that others can lighten off the weight on your shoulders especially when it comes to accomplishing your goals.

You are at your best whenever you are expressing generosity, accepting and comforting other people especially when they needed it the most as well as having an attitude of gratitude. Your life purpose can be express through service and love which is why even if you are inclined to struggle with being self – righteous or co – dependent. Your primary destiny expression purpose is to live a nurturing path, compassionate detachment, accepting other people for who they are and sharing your beautiful dreams to make the world a better place.

Chapter Seven: Destiny Expression Numbers 5, 6, 7, 8 and 9

Destiny Expression Number 7

In numerology, this destiny number calls you to create a sense of faith and trust in yourself to find the answers to your questions about the meaning of your life and life in general. Your primary goal is to search information and be able to analyze or interpret it. One of your main things is learning about spirituality and gaining worldly wisdom. You may be the kind of person who contemplates, and you just have a passion for seeking knowledge and finding the truth as this feed your soul and give you that sense of inner wisdom.

The destiny expression number 7 sets you up in a path wherein you will have to continuously get closer to finding your true 'self' through contemplating life's biggest questions. This is the reason why you always need to have considerable amount of alone time or isolate yourself from time to time (though not all the time) because this is how you will reconnect to your inner spirituality.

There are two sides pulling you in opposite direction; the first one is analyzing information and data, and the second is that you are highly intuitive so it's like mind versus heart for you all the time. This is why you are called to be able to integrate these two elements – the rational and

Chapter Seven: Destiny Expression Numbers 5, 6, 7, 8 and 9

the irrational; your intuition and intellect so that you can get the best of both worlds.

You must not totally withdraw yourself from the world just to gain clarity about yourself or contemplate life's deepest questions because that's not what the seven destiny expression number has set you out for. The best use of you skills and talents is through cultivating knowledge and turn that idea to something practical. You are at your best whenever you find a passion that you're really into. You are on a different wavelength compared to most people which could be the reason why you're sometimes misunderstood or perhaps misread. You can also seem to be distant when in fact you're somewhat busy contemplating the world around you as well as connecting and pondering with your inner self.

One of the red flags you would want to avoid is your sharp tongue because your words may hurt other people without you even knowing it. One of the best qualities you have is your observation skills and strong spirituality in any shape or form. You are also inclined to become quite superficial, skeptic, cynic as well as depression since you are a gentle soul which means that you are called to share your wisdom and truth with the world.

Chapter Seven: Destiny Expression Numbers 5, 6, 7, 8 and 9

Destiny Expression Number 8

In numerology, this destiny number calls you to create financial security for yourself as this will allow you to have freedom and make the world a better place. This number calls you to learn self – mastery and sets you a life path that revolves around establishing a business, an organization, or a career that is related to finances. One of your primary purposes also includes achieving personal power, authority as well as ethics.

As an eight destiny expression, you must learn how to be relentless and you must also be a master of whatever endeavor you pursue. You must learn how to use all your talents and abilities so that you can become financially abundant and be able to generously share your wealth to other people.

Once you realized that you are here to achieve abundance and also gain power, and you execute upon this realization, it will be much easier for you to fulfill what you are destined to do.

The main red flag you need to watch out for is over – the – top authority. You are prone to becoming a control freak, greedy, and ruthless if you don't become aware of it at

Chapter Seven: Destiny Expression Numbers 5, 6, 7, 8 and 9

the onset. What you can do to counter all of these negative sides of yours is to just focus on creating abundance, staying humble, and sharing your blessings to others. Generosity is the antidote to greediness and humility is the antidote to boastfulness caused by being in power or in authority; that's how you can keep things balance for you.

Keep in mind that even if you are a business – minded kind of person, you should still have sentiment for other people's needs. You are called to learn how to become charismatic and confident without becoming corrupted or greedy of wealth and power. And because you are bound to be rich in your lifetime, this also means that you have a responsibility to give - back and improve the lives of others especially the unfortunate.

You are a powerhouse and you give off that opinionated and directive manner which is why sometimes people misunderstood you as someone who doesn't care about others and only care about money or gaining authority. You are at your best when you create wealth for yourself and be able to balance it out through philanthropy. If you learn that the purpose of money is to give it away generously and genuinely then you are fulfilling your mission.

Chapter Seven: Destiny Expression Numbers 5, 6, 7, 8 and 9

Another thing you should watch out for is that you should never prioritize wealth and power over relationships. Learn how to be balance and still make time especially for the important things in life. Try not to be stubborn and welcome other people's opinion or advice because they may help you build your empire.

You must also learn how to empower yourself as this will open the gates for you in achieving what the destiny expression number eight has in store. If you do learn how to empower yourself, there will be lots of opportunities waiting for you that will make you step up or also be stepped on, and this is because the number 8 is a testing number. The destiny expression number is also an amplifier which means that you will encounter greater intensity than other people especially if it involves money and power. You are set up for a life where you need to overcome many challenges and seemingly insurmountable roadblocks along the way to make your dent in the universe.

There are many individuals with the eight destiny expression number that struggles with finances. Now I know all of us have to deal with finances one way or another but for an eight like you, it is a constant theme and this is the arena where you will be tested.

Chapter Seven: Destiny Expression Numbers 5, 6, 7, 8 and 9

First and foremost, if you want to live up to your destiny expression number, you must learn how to empower yourself and establish personal boundaries in order for you to make the most out of the opportunities around you. Only then will you be able to access the financial abundance as well as material desires. Expect lots of challenges along the way as these are what will make you wiser, stronger and also humble once you already possess immeasurable wealth and power.

Destiny Expression Number 9

In numerology, this destiny number calls you to achieve a higher level of consciousness so that you can teach others how to achieve theirs. You are a humanitarian, and your primary purposes revolve around finding your own spiritual path and also love others unconditionally in any aspect of your life.

You are also a hopeless romantic and can often set yourself up for frustrations especially if you or other people don't live up to your expectations or ideals. You are at your best whenever you tap into your creativity, selflessness as well as emotional sensitivity.
You must learn to accept that other people may often find your ideas absurd and somewhat 'impossible' to do. Keep in

Chapter Seven: Destiny Expression Numbers 5, 6, 7, 8 and 9

mind that the destiny expression number nine calls you to heal other people's emotional wounds or scars as well as yours without any form of resentment. You must also learn to let go of the past without being bitter about it. What this destiny expression number set up for you is to learn how to give without expecting anything in return whether it is in an intangible or tangible form.

One of the struggles you may encounter is resentment, not being able to let go of the past, and tolerance. Ultimately, what you are here to learn is how to be in the present moment, surrender to the past, and have an open heart and mind. If ever you have had family enmeshment, you are called to let all of that go through having the courage to step out or say 'no' from time to time so that you can find your own identity. You must learn how to healthily engage with your family but also detach yourself from what they would want you to become otherwise you'll never find your true calling, and you may also feel overly responsible for them.

You will also find that you can reach out more to people if you learn how to listen to them rather than as someone who gives advice or 'preach.' Keep in mind that you possess a rather intimidating quality despite of having a giving heart which is why you should be careful about how

Chapter Seven: Destiny Expression Numbers 5, 6, 7, 8 and 9

you frame your dialogues with others so as not to make them feel like you are patronizing them. Some people may also see you as someone who is un – approachable or even arrogant. Sometimes others will think of you as someone who knows or have it all which is why you may find it hard to ask for support or help because people see you as someone who have it all figured out. The destiny expression number nine sets you up for a life with multi – faceted opportunities to heal your own emotional wounds and that of others. You are here to reach out to people and learn the art of giving and also receiving.

Chapter Seven: Destiny Expression Numbers 5, 6, 7, 8 and 9

Chapter Eight: Personal Year Numbers 1, 2 and 3

Personal year numbers in numerology will guide you as to what to do in the current year. It will serve as your map as to the things that are favorable to you in any aspect of your life. This chapter will cover personal year numbers 1, 2 and 3.

Personal Year Number One

When your numerology number falls on personal year number one, you can expect lots of changes. It's all about changes, new opportunities, fresh start or new

Chapter Eight: Personal Year Numbers 1, 2 and 3

beginnings for you. Everything will be in alignment for you particularly in terms of doing something that will benefit you in the years to come. Needless to say, it is the year that will pave way for you to achieve more success in the future or open up more opportunities in your life.

For instance, if you have been thinking about travelling, switching a career, or perhaps starting a new business, this is the time to pursue that since your personal year will be favorable for you.

The number one is about venture and motivation, so if personal year number one is in your numerology chart or profile then it is calling you to keep moving forward with your endeavors and not be swayed by other people's opinion. You must also tap into your uniqueness since the numbers align for you; this could mean that if you're thinking about changing personal things about you like your style, your look, letting go of some people that you feel aren't helping you grow, or if you are thinking about changing status from single to in a relationship then this is the right time for you.

This is also the year for you to be sort of a rebel in terms of not following the status quo or not minding other people's opinion. So for instance, if your friends or family is telling you that your idea in mind sounds crazy, too bold, or

Chapter Eight: Personal Year Numbers 1, 2 and 3

maybe risky, this is the time for you to actually push through with it and not think straight because again the numbers are in your favor.

The personal year number one gives you the chance to start on something new that will impact you greatly in the next nine years of your life (since nine in numerology denotes completion). This is the time to set the trajectory of your life so for instance, you wanted to start a business, then this is the time for you to build connections or build a new out – of – the – box unconventional product as you will most likely get lucky with it which can set the tone for the succeeding years.

You are also called to clearly define your visions and goals since you will be starting something new, of course you don't want to start off with the wrong foot which is why you must clear your mind and really decide what you would want to do and commit yourself to doing that. This is the year to start taking risks, and mustering the courage to make a change. As you may know, sometimes it's really hard to make a change or to go into a new unfamiliar direction so be ready to accept that it would be quite difficult at first to let go of past things or circumstances so that you can move forward and start anew.

Chapter Eight: Personal Year Numbers 1, 2 and 3

This is also not the year to find love, get into marriage, or have fun because it's all about self – empowerment. Personal year number one calls you to stay motivated, stay empowered, and focus on self – improvement.

Personal Year Number Two

When your numerology number falls on personal year number two, you can expect being in a harmonious disposition in life. This means that you will get to create new friendships that will nurture you and people will be on your side. It calls you to also give the people around you or those who sided with you the love they deserve.

This is the perfect year to find a partner or a soul mate. You may find someone who can connect with you on a deep level or on a personal level. This is the right time to date and be on the lookout for relationship opportunities as you may come across someone who is meant to be with you. This is also the right time to get married as it will set the tone for your marriage to have a lovable, romantic, and giving atmosphere.

This is also the year to empower yourself as you may come across people criticizing you or bring you down but don't take it personally because the energy of the personal year number two is just really set up that way so don't doubt yourself and just brush off all those petty side comments you may hear from others.

Personal year number two is also about acquiring more financial abundance which means that you or your family/ partner may get to have more opportunities to earn money. This is also a great year for those of you who are musically inclined (musicians, songwriters, etc.) or if you want to learn how to play an instrument, start a musical project or get into the music scene if you are an artist because the number is in your favor. Numbers two and eleven are all about rhythm so if you have something musically related then this year will bring it to fruition. Personal year number two also gives off that beautiful vibes which means that it's the perfect time to repaint or redecorate your home, or add something that will make your environment more beautiful.

The energy of personal year number two is all about diplomacy, harmony, embracing and loving other people. It's all about relationships, environment, finances, and even personal care.

Chapter Eight: Personal Year Numbers 1, 2 and 3

Personal Year Number Three

When your numerology number falls on personal year number three, then brace yourself because this year will bring you lots of fun and happiness! You are inclined to get into a social circle. The energy of the number three is all about communication and the need to be talkative which is why you may find yourself going out all the time and meeting new people.

This is also the time to start doing creative projects whether it is in music, arts, film etc. or whatever kind of creativity you would want to do in your life as you will most likely see fruition. This personal year will enhance your creative abilities and give you an edge since the number is in your favor.

This year is all about having fun and not about creating foundation or doing something intense for yourself; it's all about loosening up and enjoyment. You will most likely realize that you also need to go out and have some fun as part of your self – care. On the flipside, this is not the year to start building a business as it may go to shambles or most likely will not come into fruition. It's all about being light – hearted and communicating to people and not doing something too productive, so to speak.

Chapter Eight: Personal Year Numbers 1, 2 and 3

The personal year number three favors those who are in artistic endeavors such as writing, performing, singing, film, comedy etc. as it's all about liberation and socialization in a fun way. This is also the perfect time for you to upgrade your style or your appearance. You will also be luckier this year and you may find more abundance especially if you are starting something that involves creativity or creative arts. Perhaps you may get discovered if you are trying to be an artist, or you will get to inspire people in the creative field that will bring you abundance.

A word of caution though since this year is all about coming out of the shell, you are prone to becoming over – indulgent or reckless; try to have some fun and get along with as many people as you can but still have some self – discipline and self – care. Take care of your health and just don't have too much fun to the point of excessiveness as what they always say, "anything in excess is bad" so try to be balance about it. You are in a light – hearted disposition which means you should also be careful when it comes to other people's feelings as they may be going through some stage in their life and could offend them in some way. Personal year number three is a great time to be optimistic, to laugh and have fun as well as soaking in that happy energy around you.

Chapter Eight: Personal Year Numbers 1, 2 and 3

Chapter Nine: Personal Year Numbers 4, 5 and 6

This chapter will cover personal year numbers 4, 5 and 6.

Personal Year Number Four

When your numerology number falls on personal year number four, this means that it's rebuilding time! You had so much fun in personal year number three but this time, you have to come back to your senses and start re-

Chapter Nine: Personal Year Numbers 4, 5 and 6

focusing things again and get things done so that you can prepare yourself for personal year number five. This is all about going back to who you are or perhaps not let everything be loose and fun just like what you did in year three.

For instance, if you think you are lacking in terms of money, then this is the time to start saving or investing and setting up that solid foundation for your financial life. If you have had trouble in your relationships, this is the time to maybe seek guidance or counsel so that you can put things into perspective – it's all about going back to the things that are important to you or that you value the most.

This is also a great year to start a business since the number four is business – oriented and it's all about building or establishing. This is also not the year for you to have fun, you have to focus on achieving the goals you set out to do otherwise you're just going to keep retracting or rebuilding. The energy of the number four brings about grounded - ness which can be helpful when you are trying to make your ideas on point. For instance, you wanted to pursue a career in acting, you are likely to think about how you can achieve your goal on a practical level and you will be bound to focus more on what you can improve on or the kind of image you will build.

Chapter Nine: Personal Year Numbers 4, 5 and 6

You have to clearly define what you value the most and what is not. You need to set your priorities straight.

Expect that you will have to work hard, if not harder this year since you are trying to build something. You are expected to tap into your reliability, logic and practicality. You are called to see things from a practical point of view and not be too idealistic so that you can finish the tasks you set out to do. You need to get aligned again with yourself and have some form of self – discipline because that's what will set you up for the next personal year which is five. This year will also make you more self – secured which means you will keep your job (hopefully), you won't lose anything in terms of finances or career etc. The energy that personal year number four gives off is that whatever you put yourself into will grow and bring into fruition.

Personal Year Number Five

When your numerology number falls on personal year number five, this year denotes that you need to experience some form of dramatic changes. The number five is the middle number and indicates that you are in the transitional stage from the start to the end of the nine year cycle. You are also bound to travel a lot whether short trips or for extended periods. You may also feel scattered in terms

Chapter Nine: Personal Year Numbers 4, 5 and 6

of your energy which means that you can be a jack of all trades, so to speak. However, don't let this feeling fool you because you still have to focus on the goals you set out to do, so try not to get too distracted by doing other things that aren't that important to you. What you can do is to center your focus and emotions are to exercise or do something that will keep your eyes on the target.

This year will bring you lots of expansion or transformation opportunities for you, which means it can be both fun and productive. You are inclined to grow and develop but you must learn to put limitations as well. It's also a good time to gamble because the number five is all about taking risks but still it is better if you take calculated risks. Luck is pretty much on your side in terms of gambling. It's also a great year to upsell yourself whether it is in relation to your business, finding new clients, or even getting a promotion/ raise from your employer.

The personal year number five also brings chaos but in an organized way. It's ironic but that's the kind of energy that number five is going to give off for you. It's like that quote or saying "when things are falling apart, they're actually falling into place."It's also a great year to create new friendships and relationships just like what you have

Chapter Nine: Personal Year Numbers 4, 5 and 6

experience in your personal year one since you are in the middle axis of the nine year cycle.

Personal Year Number Six

When your numerology number falls on personal year number six, it's going to be all about your family and also domestication. This year also denotes that you will have to carry lots of responsibilities especially when it comes to your family. One of the benefits that personal year number six will give you is heightened sense of creativity. Most individuals under this personal year start or see their business grow, or they embark on a creative project whether it is in oral or written form, in music, online presence etc. Use this to your advantage and tap into your creative side because the number is in your favor.

The number six is also the best year for mothers or those who are about to become a mom because this is the time where most moms have that sense of being really kind to their child/ children. The number six figure looks a lot like a pregnant woman if you look at the figure of the number six which is why it is all about motherhood, family and nurturing. This is also the time for women who are trying to get pregnant since the number is in your favor and you will have a better chance of bearing a child if you've been trying

Chapter Nine: Personal Year Numbers 4, 5 and 6

for quite some time. On the flipside, you may also experience some sort of drama within your family so just try to be balance and get along with them. It's also a great time for your employees/ subordinate (if any) because you will feel very close to them and you will help nurture one another. You are also bound to do some humanitarian work as you will feel very generous in your six personal year.

Chapter Ten: Personal Years Numbers 7, 8 and 9

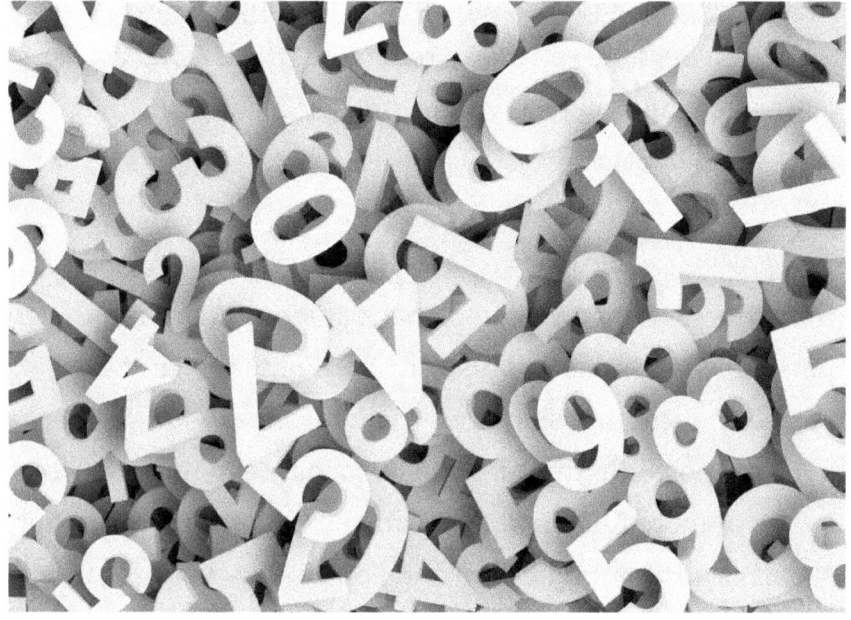

This chapter will cover personal year numbers 7, 8 and 9.

Personal Year Number Seven

When your numerology number falls on personal year number seven it denotes that you are on a pause. What this means is that this is the year wherein you will have to look back at the lesson you've learned from the previous year, and dig deep into your outlook of life in general. Some numerologist calls this as the "philosophy year."

Chapter Ten: Personal Year Numbers 7, 8 and 9

Most individuals experience some sort of epiphany or just a really profound realization that will most likely help them in the future. This is the time for you to reflect and really ask the tough question of life, or simply look back at what you've done so far and remember the lessons you've learned as this will help you in creating a better life in the next years to come.

What you can do is to write down all your deepest thoughts so that you can look back at it one day. This personal year number is also all about faith which means you may encounter situations that will show you that there's a higher power in this life. This personal year also calls you to spend more time in nature or do some form of meditation since it's all about reflection and spirituality. You will feel very attune with yourself and connected with the universe or the world in general if you are in nature.
This is the year to focus on your core, on your truth and who you really are deep down. Your faith will be tested on this personal year.

Personal Year Number Eight

When your numerology number falls on personal year number eight it denotes that you are already at the point where all your labor, hardwork and desires will come to fruition or at least it is heading you towards the direction of success. This is the year that you will be rewarded whether in your work, business, money, creative endeavor, or other aspects of your life where you worked hard on for years. You will most likely get new opportunities, or if you are working you may get promoted/ transferred to your desired department/ get a raise etc. Personal year number eight is all about getting recognized especially in your work. It's also a karmic year which means you may encounter challenges along the way, or whatever things you did the past few years haunt you.

In terms of money, you will have a better luck in improving your finances and since the number eight is all about wealth, it will bring you financial stability and agility. This is a great year to start or invest in a business, in stocks, in real estate or in other forms of assets as it may bring you wealth and fortune. It will be a year full of rewards for you but if for some reason you don't receive anything from the work you did in the past then that could denote that that particular endeavor or path is not for you, so be aware of

Chapter Ten: Personal Year Numbers 7, 8 and 9

that as well. The personal year number eight is the best year for business. Corporations like Apple Inc. raked in billions in revenue during the company's eight personal year; the number eight is very much attune to wealth and fortune.

Personal Year Number Nine

When your numerology number falls on personal year number nine it denotes that you are already at the end of your personal year cycle. The number nine is all about completion which means that this is the time to let go. Expect this year to be quite dramatic, internally speaking because this is the time when you will have to experience some form of internal change. You will start to reflect back on the things you did, the relationships you've built, the improvements and desires you've achieved over the last few years if they are worth continuing in your next journey.

In romantic relationships, this is usually where lots of breakups occur. In terms of career, it is also the time where most people either get fired from their job or choose a different career path. The things you have once prioritized usually end during the nine personal year because this is the year of preparing for a new beginning. Before you enter another 9 year cycle and go back to personal year number one, you will have to end some things, desires, or relationships to perhaps venture out on a better path or cater your new agenda. This year is all about completion which means you will most likely finish off everything you have started whatever that may be whether it's graduating from college, getting married, moving out, or finishing a particular project etc. The number nine carries with it an energy of prestige, abundance, and luck. If personal year number eight is all about fruition, the number nine is all about that added X factor that will take you further to the next level. Most numerologists agree that this is also the year for you to 'clean out your closet' both literally and figuratively because you don't want to carry with you the same energy you've had for the past nine years otherwise it will be hard for you to make way for the revitalized energy that personal year number one will bring. Get rid of the stuff that you don't need, and just keep the ones you think will be useful to you.

Conclusion

It's time to restart your life and reset your priorities but keep in mind that this is just a guide to prepare you for the real change that will happen to your life. Changes and transitions will always occur, so let numerology guide you to tap into your higher being and open life's endless possibilities!

Index

abundance 56, 57, 58, 71, 92, 93, 95, 102, 104, 115

ancient systems 4, 11, 60

born on 22, 28, 29, 33, 34, 40, 44, 45, 49, 55, 59, 60, 64, 65

challenge 32, 46, 56, 71, 78, 81

creative 14, 17, 19, 21, 29, 30, 31, 32, 36, 61, 67, 69, 73, 78, 103, 104, 109, 113

creativity 14, 17, 32, 63, 66, 69, 95, 103, 104, 109

date 3, 2, 5, 6, 7, 8, 101, 123

destiny expression ... 4, 5, 8, 9, 11, 76, 77, 78, 79, 80, 82, 83, 85, 86, 87, 88, 89, 90, 91, 92, 94, 95, 96, 97

digits 6, 11

dreams 14, 16, 21, 62, 76, 83, 84, 89

emotional wounds 37, 96, 97

energy 21, 24, 42, 43, 44, 45, 68, 69, 71, 74, 86, 101, 102, 103, 104, 106, 107, 108, 115

experience 14, 16, 17, 23, 25, 30, 32, 35, 38, 40, 41, 42, 45, 58, 60, 61, 62, 69, 72, 86, 107, 108, 109, 112, 114

family 15, 31, 37, 38, 39, 45, 57, 58, 62, 63, 79, 82, 86, 88, 96, 99, 102, 109

fear 17, 43, 44

focus 15, 18, 21, 24, 43, 72, 74, 79, 81, 88, 93, 101, 106, 108, 112

Fortunate Colors 22, 28, 33, 39, 44, 48, 55, 59, 64

freedom 40, 42, 43, 85, 86, 87, 92

fulfillment. 18

groups 2, 79

happiness .... 71, 80, 103 harmonizer 24, 79

humanitarian 64, 95, 110

independence 17, 77

life path 3, 4, 5, 6, 7, 8, 10, 11, 13, 14, 15, 16, 17, 18, 19, 20, 21, 23, 24, 26, 27, 28, 29, 30, 31, 32, 33, 35, 36, 38, 39, 40, 42, 43, 45, 46, 47, 50, 51, 52, 54, 55, 56, 57, 58, 61, 62, 63, 66, 67, 68, 69, 70, 71, 72, 73, 75, 78, 86, 87, 88, 89, 92, 123

love 23, 24, 25, 26, 27, 29, 36, 41, 56, 58, 67, 69, 70, 73, 78, 88, 89, 95, 101

Lucky days 22, 28, 33, 39, 44, 48, 55, 59, 64

Lucky Gems/ Jewels 22, 28, 33, 39, 44, 48, 55, 59, 64

Master 1, 7, 6, 7, 10, 11, 54, 66, 68, 70, 72

mission 5, 21, 69, 70, 72, 73, 74, 93

money 2, 38, 56, 57, 58, 93, 94, 102, 106, 113

number.... 4, 2, 4, 5, 6, 7, 8, 9, 10, 11, 13, 14, 15, 20, 21, 23, 24, 26, 27, 29, 30, 35, 36, 40, 45, 47, 50, 54, 55, 56, 60, 66, 67, 68, 70, 71, 72, 73, 74, 75, 76, 77, 78, 79, 80, 81, 82, 83, 85, 86, 87, 88, 90, 91, 92, 94, 95, 96, 97, 98, 99, 100, 101, 102, 103, 104, 105, 106, 107, 108, 109, 111, 112, 113, 114, 120, 121, 123

numerologists 2, 115

numerology 3, 4, 1, 3, 4, 5, 6, 8, 11, 29, 50, 56, 60, 66, 76, 78, 80, 82, 85, 87, 90, 92, 95, 98, 99, 100, 101, 102, 105, 107, 109, 111, 113, 114, 115, 121, 122, 123

numerology profile 5

open 23, 26, 53, 54, 62, 79, 94, 96, 99, 115

passive 79

personal 11, 20, 23, 28, 41, 50, 56, 58, 75, 80, 92, 95, 98, 99, 100, 101, 102, 103, 105, 107, 108, 109, 110, 111, 112, 113, 114

positivity 80

professional .... 20, 23, 36 purpose 3, 4, 1, 3, 4, 9, 12, 14, 16, 35, 37, 40, 45, 50, 53, 61, 64, 66, 69, 70, 72, 73, 77, 78, 79, 80, 82, 87, 89, 93

Pythagorean Numerology Chart 9

red flag 19, 25, 57, 79, 92

relationship 20, 41, 42, 53, 56, 58, 78, 99, 101

relationships 31, 53, 60, 79, 86, 94, 102, 106, 108, 114

struggle 19, 21, 27, 31, 38, 43, 53, 54, 57, 58, 63, 83, 89

success 18, 31, 71, 78, 83, 88, 99, 113, 120

superficial 53, 54, 91

trait 45, 47

trials 35, 77, 88

universe 3, 4, 17, 21, 94, 112, 123

value 17, 45, 58, 82, 106

wisdom 4, 52, 54, 60, 61, 63, 72, 81, 90, 91, 123

PHOTO REFERENCES

Page 1 Photo by user numerologysign via Flickr.com

https://www.flickr.com/photos/numerologysign/41803459581/in/photostream/

Page 4 Photo by user Tom Blackwell via Flickr.com

https://www.flickr.com/photos/tjblackwell/6849008278/

Page 13 Photo by user numerologysign via Flickr.com

https://www.flickr.com/photos/numerologysign/26935142127/

Page 35 Photo by user Dave Pearce via Flickr.com,

https://www.flickr.com/photos/davebass5/12703413374/

Page 50 Photo by user Telping via Flickr.com

https://www.flickr.com/photos/34247743@N07/6495318015/

Page 66 Photo by user Alan Bloom via Flickr.com

https://www.flickr.com/photos/alan_bloom/8713096731/

Page 76 Photo by user Duncan C via Flickr.com,

https://www.flickr.com/photos/duncan/4568047884/

Page 85 Photo by user Antonio Malara via Flickr.com, https://www.flickr.com/photos/biappi/2398692449/

Page 98 Photo by user Lergik via Flickr.com, https://www.flickr.com/photos/lergik/2894259671/

Page 105 Photo by user Geralt via Pixabay.com, https://pixabay.com/en/pay-digit-number-fill-count-mass-1036469/

Page 110 Photo by user TeroVesalainan via Pixabay.com, https://pixabay.com/en/target-goal-success-dart-board-1955257/

REFERENCES

What's a Life-Path Number? - Horoscope.com

https://www.horoscope.com/us/horoscopes/numerology/index-horoscope-numerology.aspx

Numerology: The Basics of Pythagorean Numerology

http://www.astrology-numerology.com/numerology.html

Numerology: What is Numerology? And How Does it Work? - TheLawofAttraction

http://www.thelawofattraction.com/what-is-numerology/

The Basics of Numerology: How to Calculate Your Life Path and Destiny Numbers - Allure.com

https://www.allure.com/story/numerology-how-to-calculate-life-path-destiny-number

Why you're about to get super into numerology - TheFader.com

http://www.thefader.com/2018/04/05/numerology-astrology-popular-spiritual-practices

Numerology as Sacred Language & Numbers' Deeper Meaning - Kasamba.com

https://www.kasamba.com/numerology/numbers-meanings/

Numerology of the Birthdate - Pateo.nl

http://www.pateo.nl/PDF/Birthdate.pdf

Cheiro's Book of Numbers - GlobalChalet.net

http://library.globalchalet.net/Authors/Cheiro/Book%20of%20Numbers.pdf

Numerology: Guide to a Happy Life - Celiawardwallace.com

http://celiawardwallace.com/downloads/the-superfly-collection/Numerology-Guide-to-a-Happy-Life-e-book-by-Kari-Samuels.pdf

The Secret Science of Numerology: The Hidden Meaning of Numbers - MysticKnowledge.org

http://www.mysticknowledge.org/The_Secret_Science_of_Numerology-_Shirley_Blackwell_Lawrence.pdf

www.ingramcontent.com/pod-product-compliance
Lightning Source LLC
LaVergne TN
LVHW051840080426
835512LV00018B/2981